Breath of Life

Breath

GOD AS SPIRIT IN JUDAISM

of Life

RABBI RACHEL TIMONER

May you be inspired.
Rachel

a PARACLETE GUIDE

PARACLETE PRESS
BREWSTER, MASSACHUSETTS

Breath of Life: God as Spirit in Judaism

2011   First Printing

Copyright © 2011 by Rabbi Rachel Timoner

ISBN 978-1-55725-704-8

Unless otherwise designated, all Scripture references are the author's translations based on the JPS Hebrew-English Tanakh by the Jewish Publication Society, copyright 1999. Substantive and stylistic changes were made where necessary.

Scripture references designated NRSV are taken from the New Revised Standard Version Bible, copyright © 1989 by the Division of Education of the National Council of Churches of Christ in the U.S.A., and are used by permission. All rights reserved.

Library of Congress Cataloging-in-Publication Data

Timoner, Rachel, 1970-
  Breath of life : God as spirit in Judaism / Rachel Timoner.
    p. cm.
  Includes bibliographical references.
  ISBN 978-1-55725-704-8 (paper back)
  1. God (Judaism) 2. Bible. O.T.—Criticism, interpretation, etc. 3. Rabbinical literature—History and criticism. I. Title.
  BM610.T56 2011
  296.3'11—dc23
                            2011032027

10 9 8 7 6 5 4 3 2 1

Published by Paraclete Press
Brewster, Massachusetts
www.paracletepress.com
Printed in the United States of America

*T*o my three loves

Contents

Introduction

I OFTEN FIND MYSELF IN THE STRANGE POSITION OF DEFENDING GOD. As a rabbi, I encounter many people who think of God as a quaint throwback to earlier times, a fantasy that sensible people gave up in the twentieth century. They are usually too polite to ask: "Don't you know about the Big Bang and evolution? Do you really believe there's a big man up there in the clouds controlling our world?"

In our era of science and technology, when humanity has mastered so much of our world and can explain many previously mysterious phenomena, belief in God seems antiquated to some—or stubborn. Like the child with her hands clamped over her ears who does not want to hear that it's bedtime, those of us who still talk about God are accused of shutting out the facts.

Some people I talk to do not trust organized religion for its contribution to war and human conflict, and for the times when religious institutions have placated suffering populations or promoted discrimination rather than changing unjust conditions. Some who are angry at religion think of belief in God not only as misleading but also as dangerous. I find that sometimes just using the word *God* carries the risk of losing my listeners, who will assume that I'm a different kind of person than they are. They will hear in that one word the message that I'm a Believer, capital *B*, someone who has stopped thinking because she knows she has all of the answers.

What's strange about this position is that I'm not very different from my wary listeners. I am fascinated by science, intrigued by the latest theories about our universe. If anything, I think too much, employ reason to a fault. I, like them, have more questions than answers. I too am critical of the role that religious institutions have played in perpetuating human suffering and war, but I also know that religion has given meaning to countless lives, including my own. There are hundreds of thousands of people working today to alleviate poverty and fight injustice because they were inspired by their religious traditions to do so. At its best, institutional religion demands that we reach for the very best we have within us, striving to create human societies grounded in justice and seeking peace.

I grew up in a home with little conversation about God but with constant conversation about politics. My parents sent me to prepare for bat mitzvah because that's what good Reform Jews did, but what they really wanted me to be was the junior senator from the state of Florida. I found no meaningful inquiry about God in my Miami synagogue of the 1980s. No one would expect that the quiet young woman who dropped out of synagogue life after becoming bat mitzvah, the Yale political science major, would be on this side of the God conversation.

I have no grand tale to offer here, no pivotal epiphany. It's just that I began to pay attention to the experience of being alive, started to ask questions about the purpose of my life, and felt drawn to dig beneath the surface for meaning. There was a camping trip in a Southwest canyon, walking out by myself on the path, a stark blue sky colliding with the jagged edges of red rock cliffs, enormous crunchy black beetles scuttling across the road, trees rustling all around, birds swooping, and the motion of river nearby but out of sight. A sudden feeling of joy, of floating, of utter belonging. Sky and cloud and cliff and grass and river, tree and wind and leaf and rock and bird—all intimate cousins, belonging to each other and to me from before time and again now. I saw that we are all part of a greater oneness. I felt it; I knew it beyond questions, beyond thinking.

There was the time after my father had a stroke. The physical therapy room of the hospital. Amputees, quadriplegics, stroke victims. He, down on a mat, paralyzed, afraid, trembling, trying to move his left arm. Me, eleven, crushed, panicked, trying to help. And then the noise of the room went still; a softness came between us, in the lock of our eyes, a fearlessness. And he moved, reached out his paralyzed arm, and held my hand.

There is that moment we've all experienced: looking at a night full of stars and seeing ourselves from the perspective of the dark and sparkling cosmos, suddenly so small as to be forgotten, so insignificant as to be a miracle. We feel, we sense that there is something beyond us, running through us, pulling us, holding us. For me, this isn't belief. It is knowing. I use the word *God* as the shorthand for what I know is there. The presence that we all experience. What we sense, perceive, intuit, feel beyond the material world.

When this mystery became compelling to me, I knew I needed to find my way back into a synagogue. It took me until I was twenty-four years old to gather the courage to do so, and there

I found old, familiar words and melodies pointing at these same experiences and questions, seeking after this same mystery. In the Jewish approach to the study of Torah, I found a legacy of open-ended, curious, creative inquiry into the meaning and purpose of our existence. Ten years later, I decided to become a rabbi. And here I am, writing about God, writing about spirit, writing about the Jewish tradition.

This book is part of a series by Paraclete Press about God as Spirit. While the other volumes address God as Spirit in Christian, Evangelical, and Orthodox thought, this book traces the idea of God as spirit through the Hebrew Bible from the perspective of Jewish tradition, with the hope of speaking meaningfully to both Christian and Jewish readers. Though our two heritages have a great deal in common, there are key differences in the way that we view God and read the Bible. Let us begin with some explanation about the Jewish way.

THE WORD *GOD*

What do we mean when we say "God"? When, in a moment of crisis or despair, we call out, "Please, God!" to whom are we calling? When, in relief or appreciation, we say, "Thank God!" to whom are we expressing gratitude? When we enter our houses of worship to offer the service of our hearts, whom or what are we addressing? When we question whether God exists, whom or what are we doubting? Is it the bearded king on the throne of heaven, the earth as his footstool? Is God a being: living, breathing, like us? Is God physical in any way, embodied, anthropomorphic ("shaped like a human")? Or is God strictly immaterial, ethereal, spiritual?

Nearly every English speaker on earth, regardless of religious affiliation, uses the word *God*, whether out of deep conviction or idiomatic expression, whether as referent to a specific image or in the absence of one. Christians and Jews translate our sacred texts from Hebrew, Aramaic, Greek, and Latin, and we find ourselves with this one word in English to describe the source of the universe and the sovereign of all that lives. This one word, and the fact that we share a sacred text, the Hebrew Bible, enables us to speak to one another and to feel that we understand one another. Because we have the same Scripture from which we read, we have the impression that when Christians and Jews say "God," we all mean the same thing.

But what do we mean?

In the ancient cultures out of which Judaism grew, gods looked and acted like people. They had faces, arms, hands, and genitals. They were male and female, and they coupled with one another. They became angry and needed appeasement; they had loyalties, agendas, and dramas. They were superhumans, with human traits writ large.

In the Hebrew Bible, one can see the influence of these cultures on the descriptions of God that have human attributes. God says, "Let us make the human in our image." God walks through the Garden of Eden. God saves the Israelites with a strong hand and an outstretched arm. God becomes angry; God feels compassion. In the prophet Isaiah's vision, God is sitting on a throne. This anthropomorphic God concept continues in post-Biblical Jewish tradition. In all Jewish blessings said to this day, God is referred to as *melech ha'olam*, "sovereign of the world."

However, Judaism's primary innovation was its understanding that God cannot be reduced to any thing we know—not a body, an object, or a natural force. The Tanakh (the Hebrew Bible) uses familiar imagery to appeal to people whose sole reference points were idols, but it does so to teach the very destruction of idolatry. The second of the Ten Commandments prohibits the creation of an image of God: "You shall have no other gods besides Me. You shall not make for yourself a sculptured image, or any likeness of what is in the heavens above, or on the earth below, or in the waters under the earth. You shall not bow down to them or serve them" (Exod. 20:3–5). How is it that the creation of an image of God was so offensive that it ranks in the top ten of all six hundred and thirteen *mitzvot* (commandments) that appear in Torah?

As we reach out for God, it is human instinct to make images, to shape forms, to create intermediaries that enable us to imagine what God might look like, or to evoke in us some feeling of affection or comprehension. This is the very danger that Torah is warning against, for even if we know that the image or statue or fetish is not really God, we can easily become confused and transfer in our minds some measure of God's greatness and power to the image we have created. And in so doing, we risk the illusion that God is our creation when, in reality, we are God's creation.

The problem is not with the imagery in the mind's eye. Our minds will make images forever; and the shifting, changing imagery of our vibrant imaginations helps us to relate to the ineffable. The problem is when we fix an image. When we shape God in stone or wood or paint, we exercise control over God's image and features. We tame God into something finite, as if the infinite One were within our control. We reduce God in our imagination to a thing, which impoverishes our perception of who and what God is. It is the externalized, shared, fixed image that is dangerous because it falsely limits what is infinite.

Moses Maimonides, a twelfth-century rabbi physician, was the greatest elucidator in Jewish history of the prohibition on idolatry. He teaches that to worship any created thing, or to make something a mediator between us and the Eternal One, is idolatry. Even if the use of that intermediary is to direct one's heart to the Eternal, it concretizes the intangible and stands between us and God.[1] This is why Judaism insists that God has no shape or form. This is why we must not attempt to represent God by what is found in the heavens, the earth, or the sea—for nothing that we find or know can adequately represent the unknowable One.

Since the days of Maimonides, all references to God's body are understood by Judaism as metaphor, as figurative language that enables us to relate to God. When a Jew reads of God's strong hand and outstretched arm bringing us out of Egypt, we understand the language to be poetic, describing God's might and saving power. When we remind ourselves that humanity was created in the image of God, we do not mean that God has a pinky finger, but that we have a sacred dignity about us, and we should treat one another with that in mind. When we read of Moses speaking to God *panim el panim*, "face to face," we understand Torah to be describing an unrivaled intimacy between our great prophet and the Holy One.

WHAT DO WE MEAN BY *SPIRIT*?

When we hear the phrase, "God as spirit," I would imagine that most Christians think of the Trinity, and within Trinity the Holy

Spirit. For Jews, the phrase "God as spirit" is less clear. Jews do not believe that God has three Persons. In fact, every time we pray, Jews all over the world speak our central statement of faith— *Shema Yisrael, Adonai Eloheinu, Adonai Echad.* "Hear O Israel, Adonai our God, Adonai is One" (Deut. 6:4). The oneness of God is our central and most important tenet. It would seem, then, that God as spirit is a point at which Judaism and Christianity diverge. If Jews believe in one, indivisible God, what does it mean to say, "God as spirit"?

When I first took on the project of writing this book, it was difficult to explain to other Jews, particularly other rabbis. "What are you writing?" they'd ask.

"I'm writing a book about God as spirit in Judaism."

"God *as* spirit in Judaism?" they repeated, their brows furrowed, a puzzled look in their eyes. "What does that mean? . . . What will you say?"

The phrase "God as spirit" raises concerns for Jewish listeners because it sounds Christian. Let's start with the word *as*. The word *as* sounds like God turns into different forms, one of which is spirit. As we've seen, the most important idea, after the idea that God cannot be compared to anything, is the idea that God is one. If God is one, and God is indescribable, how can God manifest in different ways? In order to make sense of the concept in Jewish terms, it helps to remember that God has many different names and faces in the Hebrew Bible and Jewish tradition. For example, during the Rabbinic period (in the first six centuries of the common era) and later, God is seen as having a feminine, indwelling presence called the *Shekhinah.* The Rabbis of the Talmud call God *HaKadosh Baruch Hu* and *HaRachaman,* meaning

"The Holy One, Blessed be He" and "The Compassionate One," among many other names. Our tradition sometimes describes God as the lord of a great army, sometimes as a parent. If we can see God in all of these different ways, we can also see God as spirit. In this light, "God as spirit" can mean spirit as a name for God, as a metaphor for God, as a possession of God, or as a human experience of God.

The next issue is the word *spirit*. The English word *spirit* comes from the Latin *spiritus*, which means "breath"—and in Latin is often associated with soul, courage, and vigor. The Latin is an adaptation from the Greek *pneuma*, meaning "breath" and "incorporeal presence," associated with consciousness, mind, and intelligence. The word *spirit* we use in English today has retained these associations, most commonly meaning the nonphysical parts of a person. Spirit is related to breath, but it is more than breath. We say "inspiration" to mean both the intake of air into our lungs and the spark of vision, idea, and motivation. While "respiration" is breathing, "aspiration" is goal or passion.

Rabbi Lawrence Hoffman writes: "What most Western thought takes as spiritual rhetoric is largely foreign to Jewish spiritual discourse. . . . The language of spirituality (like the language of theology) is a foreign implant for Jews. It is not that Jews have no ideas that correspond to . . . Christian theological topics . . . but it takes a sort of translation process to arrive at what our parallels are. . . . It is not as if Jews can't use those words, but it takes work to make them fit."[2]

Over the last thirty years, as Jewish spirituality has become increasingly popular, a growing number of Jewish leaders and writers have been working on translating the language of spirituality for Jewish use, to make the words fit. Rabbi Lawrence Kushner calls spirituality "the immediacy of God's presence." Rabbi Arthur Green defines spirituality as "the striving for life in the presence of God and the fashioning of a life of holiness appropriate to such striving." Rabbi Nancy Fuchs-Kreimer says, "Spirituality, as I understand it, is noticing the wonder, noticing that what seems disparate and confusing to us is actually whole." Rabbi Kerry Olitzky says, "Spirituality is the process through which the individual strives to meet God."[3] Through the work of these rabbis and others, the language of spirit and spirituality is now available for Jews wanting to express their experience of the holy.

As we explore the complex notion of God as spirit in Judaism through the Hebrew Bible and the Jewish commentaries on it, we will find that the language of spirit has always been present in our tradition. The Hebrew word most often translated as spirit, *ruach*, is everywhere in Torah—it appears 378 times throughout Tanakh. Onomatopoeic (rhhuu-ahhh), *ruach* is life-giving breath, a simple wind, and the spirit that animates creation. Each time our lungs fill and empty, it is *ruach* that enters and escapes. As we watch our sleeping children, it is *ruach* that lifts and lowers their resting bodies. It is *ruach* that rushes past us on a mountain crest, gently flutters the leaves of an Aspen tree, and stings our faces on a blustery winter day. According to Torah, it is *ruach* that prompts ecstatic prophecy, endows us with understanding and skill, and girds us with courage and the strength to lead. It is *ruach* that God gives us and takes away, so says Ecclesiastes. *Ruach* is beyond us, around us, and within us. It is as natural as breath and as supernatural as God's own self. *Ruach*, the creative force present at the first moment of the formation of the world, is associated with God, with nature, and with humanity.

And there is more than one Hebrew word in Tanakh that is translated as spirit. Unlike *ruach*, which is an impersonal, creative force, *neshamah* is exchanged in the nurturing relationship between Creator and created. *Neshamah* belongs to the essence of God and the essence of humanity. *Neshimah* means "breath"; *neshamah* means "soul." Our souls and our breaths are intertwined and interdependent, coming from God, dwelling in us for a short time, and returning to God each night and upon our death.

Given the Jewish evolution beyond God as body, it is easy to see why *ruach*—spirit, breath, wind—and *neshamah*—breath, soul—are such immediate concepts in relation to God in Torah. Spirit is ungraspable, invisible, without shape or form. Wind is one of the few forces that we all feel, experience, and relate to even though we cannot see it and it has no shape. We feel breath every moment of every day; we live by it, but it has no image. For a religion bound by lack of imagery in description of God, these concepts are intuitive—and fundamental.

It is therefore tempting to suggest that God in Judaism is all spirit, a universal spirit, the origin and aggregate of all spirit. But we will see that it may not be that simple. It is very rare in Tanakh for God to be compared to spirit. More often, it seems that God has spirit, or gives spirit, or takes spirit back. To say simply that God is spirit might be another reduction of the mysterious infinite One. Our words and concepts for the nonmaterial world are so few and undeveloped that we run the risk of oversimplifying with our limited vocabulary. We use words, ideas, images—all of the tools we evolved animals have to communicate—but all of these are simply our best but imperfect efforts to describe something indescribable.

When Moses, the shepherd-in-exile, allows himself to be drawn off course by the bush that is all aflame but not consumed, when he turns aside and listens, the God he encounters does not define itself as spirit.

"Who should I say sent me?" the reluctant prophet asks of the One.

"*Ehyeh asher ehyeh*" is the response. "I am that I am."

God says: I exist. You cannot comprehend me, but I exist. The Hebrew word for God is *Elohim*, the plural of an ancient Semitic word for god, *el*. The Jewish people's special name for God, the unpronounceable four-letter name that appears throughout the Hebrew Bible, hints at breath, wind, and spirit but points to a mystery beyond them. Known as the tetragrammaton, these four letters—*yod, hey, vav, hey*—are related to the verb "to be." The root of the word—*hey, vav, hey*—is the Hebrew word for the present, as in the present tense. A *yod* before a Hebrew verb in Modern Hebrew brings that verb into the future, but in Tanakh it generally shows continuing action, turning an action completed in the past into something ongoing. Therefore, it is possible to read the tetragrammaton as the present becoming forever, from "what is" to "what always will be."

Human beings like to give others names, and we are good at it. When the first human being is created, God leads it around the Garden of Eden, inviting it to name all of the animals. When we know something's name and are able to speak that name, we gain some measure of power over it. We are able to objectify what we name. In contrast, The Name, the four-letter name of God, is beyond our power of naming. Tradition has it that by the first century no one but the High Priest in Jerusalem knew how to say The Name, and he only did so one time each year, on the holiest day of the year, Yom Kippur. He did this only in the holiest city, Jerusalem, in the holiest edifice, the Holy Temple, in the holiest space within the holy Temple, the Holy of Holies. The High Priest prepared himself for days, purifying his body, his speech, and his thoughts in order to speak God's name in the Holy of Holies, the place of God's dwelling, the location of the ark of the covenant.

Rather than pronounce the tetragrammaton, Jews developed a convention of saying "Adonai," meaning "My Lord," to refer to the name. Thousands of years later, when vowels were added to the text of the Hebrew Bible, the vowels of "Adonai" were placed under the four-letter name to indicate that the reader ought to substitute "Adonai" for the name. These vowels, combined with the letters of the unpronounceable name, led to incorrect renderings such as "Jahovah." Instead, the four-letter name of God retains a mystery and power that cannot be tamed with our speech. By remaining unpronounceable, the name points to a magnitude beyond the limits of our capacity for expression. But, *if* we could hear God's name expressed, *yod-hey-vav-hey* would sound like wind, or breath, or spirit. Expressed without vowels these four letters together would be a deep, released breath, like wind moving through cliffs, like spirit hovering.

BIBLE WITH A JEWISH LENS

Putting the pieces together, we are beginning to see God from a Jewish perspective: singular, without image, with a name that hints at spirit. As we embark on this exploration of the Jewish idea of God as spirit, there are a few ideas to impart about how Jews interact with Torah. Jews don't read Torah; we delve into it. The blessing for the study of Torah describes the act as occupying oneself, as engagement. We study Torah as an archaeologist excavates a dig site. Our assumption is that the surface layer gives us only a small fraction of the treasure contained within. We seek out hints, clues, associations, metaphors, and hidden meaning. Never in Jewish history has there been only one correct reading of a verse of Torah. Every phrase, every word, is laden with possibility, and our tradition holds that multiple interpretations can coexist as true.

It is therefore important that we keep in mind that for Jews Torah does not stop at the edges of the scroll. The meaning of any word in Holy Scripture is not fixed or finite; it is shaped by both the words that surround it and the generations of interpreters that fill the white space around it. The Kabbalists, the Jewish mystics of the thirteenth to sixteenth centuries, called Torah black fire on white fire, to say that meaning is burning in the letters and in the space around them. It is not possible to understand Judaism by reading the Hebrew Bible on its own. Just as the Hebrew Bible provides only the first chapter to Christianity and is read by Christians through the lens of the New Testament, so too the Hebrew Bible provides only the first chapter to Judaism and is read by Jews through the eyes of Rabbinic Judaism: the Midrash, the Mishnah, and the Talmud, which were redacted between 200 and 600 of the Common Era. Intergenerational inquiry changed the lens through which we read the text. Each new generation adds its own questions, concerns, and perspectives. The conversation taking place across the generations itself becomes Torah.

Therefore, the Torah found in these pages is read through the lens of Jewish tradition as recorded in the centuries and millennia following the Biblical era in the writings of the early Rabbis, in the commentary of the medieval rabbis, and in the literature of modern and contemporary rabbis and scholars. Even the categories by which we will look at God as spirit in Judaism are shaped by the many generations that followed the Biblical authors.

CREATION, REVELATION, REDEMPTION

When the Rabbis of the first century of the Common Era developed the fixed prayers that were said morning and evening, they identified three central themes of the Jew's relationship to God: creation, revelation, and redemption. Morning and night in the liturgy, Jews express gratitude to God for the creation of the universe, for revelation through Torah and *mitzvot* (commandments) at Sinai, and for our liberation from Egypt, which serves as a symbol of our eternal hope for future redemption. These three themes shape the way that Jews see God. Let us take a moment to describe each of these themes, as it is through them that we will explore God as spirit in Judaism.

Creation. We look out at the vast cosmos, or we see the splash of purple in the center of a wild snapdragon, or we feel the sensations of our bodies—and we meet God. This is the relationship of creation. We exist, we experience, we wonder at what we find here, and we look for its source. We have a sense of origins, of coming from and belonging to something larger. We marvel at the intricacy, the harmony, and the balance in the ecosystems we encounter. The range and diversity of species dazzles us. This is the dimension of creation. In this book we will ask: what is the role of God as spirit in the day-by-day creation of the world?

Revelation. Given this spectacular world in which we find ourselves, how should we live? Human beings are not only a part of the unfolding drama of creation, but we are also conscious of it. We have questions. We want to learn. Not only do we want to know who made this world, but we also want to be in relation with that Who, and we sense that He/She wants to be in relation with us. Abraham heard a voice, followed it, and learned a way of life. Since then, Jews have understood ourselves to be in covenant with God, in a committed relationship of learning and action. We ask: what is our role in this world? What is a good way to live? We learn to restrain our desires in order to prevent harm to others. We learn that there is a middle path between excess and poverty and that we have obligations to others and to the weakest among us. We learn to balance between work and rest, and we learn to find harmony with the land. The word *Torah* means "teaching," or "guidance." We are always asking questions and learning with the goal of doing good. This is the dimension of revelation. In this book we ask: what is the role of God as spirit in the giving and receiving of revelation?

Redemption. When we see the splendor of the created world and seek understanding about how to live in it, we become aware that the world is not only beautiful but also broken. When we look more carefully, we see suffering, injustice, and oppression. The dimension of redemption is the commitment to give of ourselves to make the world whole again. It is the belief that God is working through us to repair what's broken and to relieve suffering. It is the belief that there will be a time when the world will be whole, when all will unite in a system of harmony and equality. It is the understanding that this is the purpose of our lives—to wonder at the majesty of creation, yes, to seek intimate relationship with the One and learn about how to live, yes, but ultimately to act in such a way that our lives are instruments of God's will to repair the broken world. Through our lives, we will contribute to the bringing of the messianic age, a time when all will be one. In this book we ask: what role does God as spirit play in the ongoing work of redemption?

As you can see, Judaism tells a story. It is a story with a beginning, a middle, and an end. In the beginning we came to be, in the middle we learn how to live, and in the end we contribute our lives toward justice and peace. Our challenge will be to find the thread of God as spirit woven through this story. What does God as spirit add to our understanding of creation, revelation, and redemption? What do each of these themes add to our understanding of God as spirit in Judaism? These three categories—creation, revelation, and redemption—existence, understanding, hope—form the Jewish personality, our understanding of God, and our sense of responsibility in the world. What, then, is the role of God as spirit in shaping who Jews are?

PART ONE

Creation: Breath of Life

1
Spirit Shaping Cosmos

*W*HEN WE BEGIN AT THE VERY BEGINNING, with the story of the creation of the world, we find a story that features God's spirit. In the deep, dark beginning of time, when all was unformed and void, *ruach Elohim*—breath, wind, spirit of God—swept over the mingled waters of heaven and earth. Chaos subsided. There was voice. There was light. Day and night, separation and order.

The word *ruach*, like so many words in Torah, is full of potential and variable meaning. Right here, in the second verse of the Hebrew Bible, we enter into the mystery of Torah's description of God. *Ruach Elohim* could be a wind created by God to subdue and divide the waters, in which case God used a natural force, an element of creation, to further creation. *Ruach Elohim* could be a breath belonging to the Holy One, like that which sustains us. Alternatively, *ruach elohim* could describe the Ineffable itself in the act of creation, spirit-God as the source of life. Or, as Everett Fox translates, *ruach Elohim* could be the "rushing-spirit of God hovering over the face of the waters."[4]

If that's so, *ruach Elohim* is not a description of God or an aspect of God but rather a possession of God. In such a view, it is not

God *as* spirit, but God *has* spirit. We find ourselves with four possibilities: God using wind to create; God breathing to create; God as spirit creating; and God's spirit as God's creative force. In the coming pages, we will try on a few of these ideas about God and *ruach*, imagining what Torah might mean to tell us about God, the origins of our universe, and ourselves.

RUACH: GOD'S CREATIVE SPIRIT

"The earth was a formless void . . . , while a wind [**ruach**—*also "spirit"*] *from God swept over the face of the waters."* (Gen. 1:2 NRSV)

Stretch back now to a time beyond memory. In the soup of origins, in the beginning of God's creating heaven and earth;[5] there was *tohu vavohu*—chaos, void, and in the words of Rabbi Bradley Artson, "emergent, unpredictable becoming."[6] There was pregnant darkness over depths of the not-yet. There was water, water waiting for life and form. And over that water hovered *ruach Elohim*. Face to face with those dark, watery depths vibrated the creator in the form of *ruach*.

The first time we meet God, God has, or is, *ruach*. Why?

What about the function of God's *ruach* places it at the opening moment of our story? From the third verse of Genesis to the end of the story of creation, there is no further mention of *ruach*. God is simply God. God speaks. God separates. God names. God decides that it is good. The word *ruach* does not appear again until chapter 7, with the great watery destruction of all that breathes. Why does God need *ruach* at the beginning?

What we see in these first verses of Torah is that God's *ruach* has a special relationship to creation, organizing chaos and bringing life from the depths. It is through God's *ruach* that God transforms uninhabitable space-time into benevolent, life-giving order. God's *ruach* here is an aspect of God that enables God to create. Shaping chaos into order is beyond what breath or wind as we know them can do. It seems that God's *ruach* here is God's spirit, and interestingly, God's spirit feminizes God.

A shapeless, formless, indescribable God is beyond our notions of gender. However, all Hebrew nouns are gendered, either feminine or masculine. Most nouns have a single gender—they are always masculine or always feminine. *Elohim*, the name for God we find in the process of creation in Genesis, is masculine. *Ruach* can be either masculine or feminine. At the birthing of the world, however, *ruach* is in feminine form. *Ruach Elohim* together become feminine just as God is bringing forth form out of the darkness, hovering over the depths to birth all of life. As a midrash describes it, in the beginning, God fluttered like a nesting dove over her fledgling chicks.[7]

The verb describing what God's spirit did at that opening moment of creation is *merachefet*, meaning "hover," "vibrate," "sweep," or "flutter." It is in the present tense. This implies that our creation is not a single event that happened 5,771-plus years ago "in the beginning," or 160,000 years ago as Homo erectus became Homo sapiens. Creation is an ongoing event. It happened in the beginning, and it happens now, in every moment. It happens in our backyards, with every blade of grass that pushes its way out of seed in dark soil. It happens every second in our bodies with the creation of new cells. It happens all around us as atoms collide and create new molecules. It is the great, continual birthing forth of the world in elaborate and intricate design.

One of the most extraordinary features of God's spirit, God's creative force, is that some of its creations also have spirit, enabling God's creations to create as well. Another midrash describes God's role in creation as that of an unparalleled artist: "A mortal may draw a picture, but the picture cannot draw a picture in turn. But when the Holy Blessed One draws a picture, God's picture makes other pictures. God made a woman, and the woman gives birth and produces others like herself."[8] Here again, God is cast in a female role, as *ruach Elohim* is in feminine form, possessing the power to create those who will in turn create. We see the role of God's *ruach* from generation to generation. It is God's *ruach* that enables God to create. God creates us, bestows upon us God's *ruach*, and enables us to create.

According to these images given to us by the Midrash, not only was God's *ruach* fluttering like a dove over her hatchlings when all was dark, formless, and void; not only is God's *ruach* the sculptor of the animating dynamic of the created order; not only does God's *ruach* continue to hover over every living thing, bringing forth millions of new creations every moment; but God's *ruach* rests on us too, giving us the extraordinary ability to create. Soon we will see how *ruach* is shared between God and humanity and serves as a creative force in human beings as well.

GOD'S SPIRIT AND THE BIG BANG

For many centuries, most Jews have understood the creation story in *Bereishit*, the Book of Genesis, to be a nonliteral, nonhistorical accounting of the beginning of the world. Rashi, Rabbi Shlomo ben Yitzchak, the most authoritative Torah commentator in all of Judaism, lived in France in the eleventh century. He said the following of Genesis 1:1: "This verse does not intend to teach the sequence of creation." Rashi parses the use of the word *bereishit*, "in the beginning," to show that chapter 1 of Genesis cannot be read as a sequential accounting of the creation of the world. One point in his proof is that the text implies that water preceded earth and gives no account of the creation of water. Rashi deduces: "You are therefore forced to admit that Scripture did not intend to teach anything of the earlier or later sequence of creation."[9] In addition, it is not at all clear that Genesis 1 is literally describing seven days of creation. Immediately following the account of creation, we read, "These are the generations of heaven and earth when they were created, on the day [*yom*] Adonai God made earth and heaven" (Gen. 2:4). If we read the word *yom* literally as one day, we have a problem: were heaven and earth created in seven days, or in one? Therefore, we are forced to conclude that *yom* is not literally a twenty-four-hour day, but a day is metaphor for an unspecific period of time.

We also find that the text can coexist with our contemporary understanding of the universe when we follow a more accurate translation of Genesis 1:1 instead of the familiar "In the beginning." What the Hebrew says (and is now reflected in most modern translations) is "When God began to create . . ." This phrase implies that the following verses are the steps God took in the creation of this earth while not precluding the earlier creation of the universe and other bodies in it.

Like poetry, the first chapters of Genesis use evocative and abbreviated language to describe where we come from. When understood metaphorically, this language need not be at odds with our latest scientific theories of the Big Bang and evolution, but instead they offer complementary wisdom about our origins and the origins of the universe we find ourselves in. If the Big Bang explains what happened, Genesis interprets what creation means.

The Big Bang theory dates the origin of our universe to roughly fifteen billion years ago.[10] In *God and the Big Bang*, Jewish scholar Daniel Matt describes the scientific understanding of the first moments of our universe. According to Matt, scientists say that the Big Bang took place in a vacuum—space had no matter but was full of potential energy particles.[11] Through a fluctuation in the energy, a vibration formed a tiny bubble—hot, dense, and smaller than a proton but with all the mass and energy of our universe.[12] As the bubble cooled, it expanded rapidly, creating the radiation of the Big Bang. For the next 300,000 years, the universe was a mixture of radiation and particles, a soup of chaotic energy, thick and opaque like fog. Finally, the universe cooled sufficiently for photons to oscillate at a lower frequency, freeing electrons to form orbits around protons and neutrons, creating stable atoms of hydrogen and helium, which would eventually form galaxies. Only then, when matter and radiation separated, did the soup thin and become transparent, and photons become visible as light.[13]

If we overlay Torah's creation story with the story from science, we might read it as follows: "In the beginning of God's creating, there was *tohu vavohu*, a chaotic soup of energy. There was thick and opaque darkness over the endless depths of the vacuum of nothing. Then *ruach Elohim merachefet al pnei hamayim*—then the spirit of God vibrated over the soup. And God said, 'Let there be light,' and matter and radiation separated, and there was light."

One of the mysteries that commentators have focused on in understanding these verses of Torah is how God created light on day one and the sun and stars on day four. Given that all of the light we see comes from the sun and the stars, what is the light created on day one? Over the millennia, rabbis have suggested that the light at the beginning was a mystical light, sparks of which are in every living thing today. Our scientific theories now tell us that in the creation of the universe there was light long before there were stars. What if the rabbis were right—what if the creation of light, the light that emerged before the sun and the stars existed, was the souling of the universe?

How might we imagine the role of *ruach Elohim*, the spirit of God, in this new/old creation story? When the spirit of God vibrated over the murky soup of chaotic energy, what happened? The word *merachefet* ("vibrates" or "oscillates") is fascinating here. All of existence oscillates—matter (in the form of subatomic particles) and energy, light and sound. Our bodies are continually oscillating in the rhythm of our heartbeat and breath. Everything around us is pulsing, beating out a steady rhythm. Often in the natural world rhythms become entrained, meaning that they find the same or related frequencies and wavelengths, to be in a kind of harmony with one another. We might read Torah to say that the oscillating spirit of God hovered over the frenzied soup of primordial energy entraining it into stable and steady vibrations of matter and radiation, from chaos to order, from darkness to light.

As we imagine God's spirit vibrating over the chaos of the early universe, we also know that the universe was expanding. Long before we knew this from astronomers, Judaism's mystics imagined it, with God's *ruach* as the cause.

BREATH OF THE WORLD

In the twelfth and thirteenth centuries in Spain, a mystical tradition arose in Judaism called Kabbalah. Through study, analysis, fasting, and pious prayer, the Kabbalists sought the mystical secrets of God and the universe hidden within Torah. One Kabbalistic interpretation of the creation story imagines God creating the universe with breath. This vision of *ruach Elohim*—a vision that aligns remarkably with the Big Bang theory—sees God breathing the universe into existence. "When a glassblower wants to produce glassware, he takes an iron blow-pipe, hollow as a reed from one end to the other, and dips it into molten glass in a crucible. Then he places the tip of the pipe in his mouth and blows, and his breath passes through the pipe to the molten glass attached to the other end. From the power of blowing, the glass expands and turns into a vessel—large or small, long or wide, spherical or rectangular, whatever the artisan desires. So God, great, mighty and awesome, powerfully breathed out a breath, and cosmic space expanded to the boundary determined by divine wisdom, until God said, 'Enough!'"[14]

Here God, like the great artist described in the previous midrash, knew the size and shape for the beginning of the cosmos, and breathed out until cosmic space expanded to the size necessary for the creation of the world. From there, God could separate light from darkness and create the world that we know. The psalmist also describes God breathing the universe into being. "By the word of the Lord the heavens were made, by the breath [*ruach*] of his mouth, all their host" (Ps. 33:6). Because this psalm draws a parallel between "word" and *ruach*, we can say that when God speaks to create the world in Genesis 1, it is God's *ruach* at work. What are words but shaped breath? In the Second Book of Samuel, David describes that power of God's breath in the creation of the world. "The foundations of the world were revealed by your roaring, Adonai; at the exhale of the breath [*nishmat ruach*] of your nostrils" (2 Sam. 22:16; Ps. 18:16).

In a moment, we will see that in Genesis humanity was created through God's breath, a breath that is both breath and spirit. Here the Kabbalists and the psalmist are imagining that it was not only humanity that was created with God's breath but also that God created the entire universe by breathing into it. From this view, the *ruach Elohim* present at the beginning of creation was God's breath sweeping like a great wind through the cosmos, expanding space so that shape, order, and eventually life could be born. As astronomers today can prove, the universe continues to expand, which allows us to imagine God continuing to breathe into the universe, not only bringing life into all creatures but also breathing existence into the cosmos.

The fact that the three concepts associated with *ruach* in the Bible—breath, wind, spirit—share the same Hebrew word indicates that they are not entirely distinct. Though we might experience them as three different phenomena, according to the Bible they are more clearly related than we might imagine. This teaches us the possibility that the relationship between our breath and the wind that blows past us, between our breath and our spirit, between our breath and God's "breath," and between our spirit and God's spirit, are all closer than we think.

A nesting dove, a stabilizing vibration, a breath sweeping through the universe: no matter what we compare it to or how we imagine it, Torah begins with the assertion that, at the first moments of creation, God's spirit was there to birth and breathe the world into life. Soon, humanity would be born into that magnificent, multifaceted world; and as we'll see, God's spirit was there to birth and breathe us too.

2
Spirit in Us

W E ARE BORN INTO A CREATED, AND continually re-created, world. By the time we become aware of the world around us, we have already been breathing since before we can remember. But there was a moment when we breathed our first breath. Where did that breath come from? What, according to Jewish tradition, is the role of God's spirit in our birthing and our breathing, our life, our sustenance, and our death? This is the subject we turn to now.

ENTER THE FIRST HUMAN

There are two accounts of the creation of human beings in Genesis. For now, let's begin with the second telling of the creation of humanity, about which we read, "The Eternal God formed the human [*adam*] of dust from the earth [*adamah*], and blew in its nostrils breath of life [*nishmat chayim*] and the human [*adam*] became a living being [*nefesh chayah*]" (Gen. 2:7).

Out of dust of the earth God formed the *adam*, the first human. Notice the relationship between the words *adam* "human being" and *adamah* "earth"—earth creature and the earth from which it comes. Here the *adam* is not yet a man named Adam. Later, when the woman is formed, he will be called Adam, and he will be male. But for now, the *adam* is a universal earth creature, preceding gender and name.

In this story of the creation of the first human being we learn that we are made from the matter of the earth, and now science confirms that we are. Carbon, hydrogen, nitrogen, calcium, oxygen, and phosphorous make up 90 percent of our bodies. Every element found in the earth's crust is also found in us. In Genesis, the human being is a creature formed from two ingredients: *adamah* ("earth") and *nishmat chayim* ("life breath").

It is the *adam*'s second ingredient that makes the *adam* different from the earth from which it was formed. This second ingredient is not just oxygen, not just air, but *nishmat chayim*, "life breath." Life breath is a mysterious combination of air and spirit breathed into us by God. We are merely made of the stuff of the earth until God forces life breath into our nostrils and we become alive. Thus, Torah teaches, the *adam* became *nefesh chayah*, "a living being." This first life breath, from God to the *adam*, is our first glimpse of the creation of a human soul. This is the first human being, made simply of earth and life breath. This is us, made of the elements of our surroundings and an enlivening kiss from God.

Nishmat Chayim is transmitted from God to the first human and to every human being, giving us a *neshamah*, a "soul." God possesses and bestows breath, soul, spirit. Humans live by it. Breath is God's intimate gift to us—not only the first breath of the first human being, not only our first breath at the moment of our birth, but all breath, every breath, a moment-by-moment touch from God enabling us to live until the next moment, and the next, and the next.

IN THE IMAGE OF GOD'S SPIRIT

God's intimate gift of life breath bestowed on each human being doesn't only keep us alive; it also makes us who we are. In the first story of the creation of humanity, we learn that God created humanity, male and female, in the image of God. "And God created a human being in God's image, in the image of God he created it, male and female God created them" (Gen. 1:27). For millennia, Jews have wrestled with what it means that humanity was created in God's image, particularly given that God has no image. We know that we do not look like God, so what does it mean to be in God's image?

One answer is that the *neshamah* that God breathes into us—this life breath, this spirit—is what makes us like God. With the life breath, God gives us a sensibility, an awareness, a consciousness that makes us in God's image. Unlike *ruach*, which is universal, the *neshamah* is unique to each individual, related to personality, to life purpose—our own personal infusion of godliness. We see it in the faces of newborns, and we can feel it in the presence of any human being when we stop long enough to really look. The gift of *ruach* and *neshamah* imparts the divine image to humanity and is the animating dynamic that makes our *nefesh*, our being, a subject, a self.

For the prophets of the Hebrew Bible, the creation of humanity is defined by this gift of spirit. The prophet Isaiah describes it this way: "Thus said God the Eternal: Who created the heavens and stretched them out, Who spread out the earth and what it brings forth, Who gives spirit to his people and all who walk on earth" (Isa. 42:5). Zechariah says: "The utterance of Adonai, Who stretched out the skies, and made firm the earth, and created man's spirit within him" (Zech. 12:1).

Hermann Cohen, a modern German philosopher, observes: "God the Creator becomes the molder of man's heart and spirit. . . . As the calling-into-being of heaven and earth is a special act of creation, so is the forming of man's spirit within him."[15] The creation of heaven is defined by stretching; the creation of earth is defined by spreading and making firm. The creation of humanity is defined by the gift of spirit. Abraham Joshua Heschel, one of the greatest rabbis of the modern era, comments: "What is stressed about man in these passages is the forming of the spirit, the grandeur of which is made manifest by its juxtaposition with heaven and earth."[16] As majestic as the stars in the sky, the colors of dawn, the clouds on the horizon; as variegated as the terrain of mountains, the coniferous forests, marsh grass, and cactus brush, in contrast to man these are all impoverished. None of them have spirit. The gift we receive is unique among all creation. It is the godliness within us, the image of divinity each of us possesses. It is what positions us between earth and heaven, between the mundane and the majestic, between creature and Creator.

Heschel observes that every human being, then, "is involved in a polarity between divine image and worthless dust." Each human being "is a duality of mysterious grandeur and pompous aridity, a vision of God and a mountain of dust." For Heschel, it is because each person is dust that "his iniquities may be forgiven" and because each person is an image of God that "righteousness is expected."[17]

Here humanity stands, a strange mixture of the mundane and the sublime. We are living among the animals but able to reach for our Creator. Here we stand, like earth because we are made of it, like God for the fact of our spirit, apart from the divine yet mirroring her.

EMBODIED SPIRIT

We are made of two worlds, of the mundane and the sublime, earth and heaven, body and spirit; but we are not divided. Our bodies and our spirits are intertwined. Judaism emphasizes the unity of body and spirit. Rather than aspire to transcend our bodies, we are called on to appreciate the miracle of our bodies in all of their functions. We are to celebrate and enjoy our bodies along with our spirits, feeling ourselves to be a single, integrated whole.

Many Jews around the world wake each morning with a blessing on our lips, thanking God for our embodiment. *Modeh ani lefanecha*: "I am grateful to You," *melech chai v'kayam*: "ever-living sovereign," *shehechezarta bi nishmati b'chemlah*: "for returning my soul [or breath] to me in graciousness," *rabah emunatecha*: "great is your faithfulness!"

In this wake-up call, said before rising, stretching, dressing, washing, even before opening our eyes, Jewish people are making an assumption. The assumption is that we wake because we have a soul. We live, we are conscious, *we are ourselves* because we have a soul. And it is our assumption that this soul comes directly from God—that, in fact, our moment of waking was the moment of the spirit's return to us from its nightly sojourn with the Eternal. Our soul's return to us is a sign of God's faith that we are worthy of the gift of life, and of God's faithfulness to keep the promise of life for us.

Judaism does not have a single theory of the soul, but in the predominant theory, the human soul has three dimensions. The first, the *neshamah*, that which God breathed into the first human's nostrils (Gen. 2:7), is the most elevated aspect of the soul, a pure light at the core of our being that returns to God each night as we sleep. In morning prayers, Jews all over the world exult, "God, the soul [*neshamah*] you have given me is pure. You created it. You formed it. You breathed it into me."

Ruach, the middle aspect of soul, the spirit or wind of Genesis 1:2, is the spirit of life, the animating force sustaining us and all that lives. Unlike *neshamah*, *ruach* transcends the individual person or body. As we see in Genesis, *ruach* is the life force present everywhere and existing independently of any single life. *Nefesh*, which most translations of the Bible render as "soul," literally means "being." *Nefesh* is more closely associated with the physical body than *ruach* or *neshamah*, grounding the ethereal aspects of soul to the material earth. *Nefesh* is also associated with heart and mind. Unlike *ruach* and *neshamah*, which we share with God, only humans and animals have a *nefesh*. Unlike *ruach*, a *nefesh* can die.

But the morning blessings do not end with gratitude for our souls. The blessings continue with gratitude for our bodies: for our eyes and ability to see, for our ability to stand and to walk, to move and to stretch, for our physical strength and stamina. There is even a special blessing we say when we first use the bathroom in the morning: *Baruch atah Adonai Eloheinu melech ha'olam, asher yatzar et ha-adam bechochmah* . . . "Blessed are You, Adonai our God, sovereign of time and space, who forms the human body in wisdom . . ." The prayer goes on to describe the intricate design of the body, with its many pathways and openings, and acknowledges that if just one of them were to fail to open or close, we would not be able to stand and offer praise before God. Lest we think that only the purity of our souls is cause for awe and gratitude, here we learn that even our body's ability to dispose of waste is God's miracle. For a Jew, there is no duality or hierarchy between body and spirit. We have no goal of transcending the body. Our bodies are holy instruments, through which we know pleasure, perceive truth, and strive toward righteous action. Without our bodies, we could not do what we are here to do—to fulfill the covenant with God and engage in *mitzvot* (commandments) to redeem our world. In Judaism, body and spirit are seamlessly integrated, interdependent, equal cause for gratitude and praise.

As Hermann Cohen explains, "The term 'spirit' primarily implies a contrast to all matter and therefore also to all physical being. But this contrast is not felt to represent an irreconcilable conflict. Spirit and matter are rather seen as interconnected in every living thing and therefore particularly in man."[18] The interconnection of spirit and body within enables us to know God, to feel and experience within ourselves a connection to God. As we learned before, we cannot analyze God into component parts. Just as there is no duality within God, there is no duality within us. In Judaism, we are not body versus spirit or spirit versus body, just as God is not body versus spirit or spirit versus body. Just as God is indivisibly One, each human being is an integrated creation, a unified whole.

BEING BREATHED: THE SPIRIT OF INTERCONNECTION

Integrated and whole as we may be, it is easy to imagine ourselves as separate from the world around us. We seem to be individual, sovereign selves, distinct and bounded from what lies beyond our skin. But when we look deeply we see that we and all life are dependent on, and made of, God's *ruach*. This means that we are made of the world around us more than we know.

A man sits in traffic on the way home from work. Thoughts rush through his head, one after the other, of the day that has just passed. He feels rushed. As he inches forward in the jam, he knows that bedtime is approaching, and his children are waiting to see him before they close their eyes for the night. Anxieties about a coming deadline gnaw at him. His back hurts; his neck is stiff. All of the conversations of the day now play out for him in his mind, and as he reviews them he weighs his words. He replays what he said, what was said to him. As the sky darkens, and he looks out at the sea of red brake lights on the road around him, the world feels narrow. His life feels narrow. Nothing feels real but the traffic, the deadlines, the thirst in his mouth, the last phone call he made, the things that were done and the things that must be done. It is almost impossible to imagine that anything else exists.

Amid the noise of pressures and desires, within the hurry to get home, beyond the growling of his stomach, it is forgivable that this man cannot notice the simple rise and fall of his chest. The coolness as the air enters his nose. The expansion when his chest fills and the contraction on release. The steady visit of breath.

Whether he is mentally transported back to the office or ahead to his kids in their pajamas, as his heart quickens with a memory of conflict or triumph, as his brow furrows at the unmoving cars ahead, this man is breathing. His body is moving in steady, involuntary rhythm.

Whether he believes in God or does not believe in God—whether he attends a house of worship, studies sacred texts, strives to do good, or does not—as long as he lives, his body is always breathing. He need not ever bring his awareness to his nose or throat or chest or abdomen. His lungs will continue their vital function; his blood will carry the oxygen from his heart to every needy cell in his body. He need not be aware of breathing at all, unless it stops. As long as his breathing remains unobstructed every second of every day, he can continue to think about his deadlines and desires.

If he has thought of it at all, most certainly this man thinks of his body as separate from the air he breathes. His body is him; he is his body. But his surroundings—the other drivers, the air he breathes—surely these are not him. Yet every three to five seconds he pulls these surroundings into himself. And every three to five seconds he pushes back into the space around him the elements released by his cells. He takes in and releases about two and a half gallons of air every minute. He is not as separate as he thinks. Because the air is absorbed into his blood and then cells, he is partially made of these surroundings.

In Psalm 104, the exultant ode to all creation, the psalmist calls out to God,

> How great are the things you have made, Adonai;
>
> You have made them all with wisdom;
>
> The earth is full of Your creations.
>
> There is the sea, vast and wide,
>
> With its creatures beyond number,
>
> Living things, small and great. . . .
>
> All of them look to You
>
> To give them their food when it is due.

Give it to them, they gather it up;

Open Your hand, they are well satisfied;

Hide your face, they are terrified;

take away their ruach,

they perish and turn again into dust;

send back your ruach, they are created,

and You renew the face of the earth. (Ps. 104:24–30)

Moment by moment God's *ruach* creates the entire majestic, symbiotic world in which we live. Moment by moment, breath by breath, we are sustained by *ruach* and we exchange *ruach* with everything around us. In sharing God's *ruach* with all of creation, we are linked with all of our surroundings. God's breath fills the world and is exchanged every moment of every day between living things, among the abundant and dazzling variety of creatures, each of which has its place, its way, and its sustenance. None of these is without purpose, each providing for another and depending on some other. This stunning world of God's creation is at once ordered and tenuous, vibrant and vulnerable.

This God who created and creates a glorious universe full of life in harmony with itself can—at any moment—pierce the rapture, empty the lungs, desiccate the wet world and fill it again. This theological statement of the moment-by-moment dependence of every one of us on God's providence is at once awesome and terrifying. It raises the specter of a cruel God, who could decide on a whim to suck us all dry. Yet it also conjures a profoundly nurturing God, who not only once-upon-a-time designed this perfect ecosystem but who, moment by moment, reassures us and breathes us with life. This is the nature of our existence—nurtured and vulnerable, protected and fragile, loved and mortal. As we'll see from the experience of Job, awareness of our mortality leads to an even greater appreciation of the preciousness of God's spirit within us.

HOW VULNERABLE WE ARE: DEPENDENCE UPON GOD'S SPIRIT

No one better understands the fragility of our lives than Job, who faced the destruction of everything and everyone he loved. In the speeches he makes about his condition, Job speaks often about God's spirit. Though he lived his whole life aware of God's blessing and sustenance, Job's suffering made him acutely aware of the tenuousness of our existence and our utter dependence on God.

Job was a man who had enjoyed exceptional wealth and good fortune in every aspect of his life: land, wealth, family, success, and status in the society. His great estate brings Job and his family fabulous wealth and access to every fine thing. They have "seven thousand sheep, three thousand camels, five hundred yoke of oxen, five hundred she-asses, and a very large household" (Job 1:3). Job was the single wealthiest man in the East. But remarkably, Job's wealth and good fortune never spoil him. After each feast or celebration, Job sanctifies himself and makes offerings to Adonai just in case he or his family has blasphemed God in their thoughts.

Job is so righteous, in fact, that God's confidence in Job spurs a member of God's entourage, the adversary, a kind of "public prosecutor" (in Hebrew the *satan*) to challenge him. (A note here about how the Hebrew Bible understands the word and character of the *satan*. In Job, the word *satan* always appears with the definite article preceding it. In other words, *satan* is not a proper noun. It is not a name, but a word that describes a role. It is not pronounced "sate-'n" but "sah-tahn," with short *a*'s and the emphasis on the second syllable.) The *satan* is the prosecutor in God's court. God is imagined sitting among a court of angels. As people come to trial before God, the court needs a prosecutor. This is the role of the *satan*. He is not a force independent of God. He is not equal in power to God. He acts under God's authority as part of God's court of angels to try and test people.

When God boasts that Job is the most righteous person in all the earth, the *satan* argues, in effect, that it's easy to be God-fearing when everything is going your way. "You have blessed his efforts so that his possessions spread out in the land. But lay your hand upon all that he has and he will surely blaspheme you to your face" (Job 1:10–11). God has such faith in Job that God consents to the test, allowing Job to suffer in a way that seems cruel. In a single day, all of Job's possessions are taken from him and his children killed. But Job, even in the depths of shock and grief, even when he is afflicted with inflammation from head to toe, even when he laments and protests his condition, he refuses to blaspheme God.

When his friends who come to comfort him suggest that Job has done some wrong to deserve his fate, Job is clear that he has done nothing to deserve his suffering. He tries to explain how vulnerable we all are. We are held in God's hand, he tells them; our fate is not our own: "In [God's] hand is every living soul and the spirit [*ruach*] of all humankind" (Job 12:10). One cannot ensure a life of blessing by doing good, Job is saying. When people suffer, it does not mean that they have done wrong. We are not in control of our own fate. God is in control of our *neshamah*, of our *ruach*, of our lives.

"As long as my spirit [*nishmati*] is in me, and God's breath [*ruach*] is in my nostrils, my lips will speak no wrong, nor my tongue utter deceit"[19] (Job 27:3–4). "As long as my breath/spirit is in me": Job knows better than anyone that his existence is hanging by a breath. There is no guarantee that in the moment that he is speaking, or in the moment that his friends are listening, they will continue to live. Our *neshamah* is on loan. "And God's spirit/breath is in my nostrils": Our *neshamah* and our *ruach* are linked. Our spirit and our breath are intertwined, interdependent. Without one, we do not have the other. If my spirit is taken from me, my breath will go as well. If my breathing ceases, my spirit will leave me too.

Job calls the *neshamah* his own, and the *ruach* God's. This is not uncommon in Tanakh, to associate the *neshamah* with the human being and the *ruach* with God. The *ruach* is a universal force from God, and the *neshamah* is the personalized form, what happens when the universal meets the individual. God shares *ruach* with all life and *neshamah* with each unique individual. Though you and I may feel the same *ruach* (wind) blowing by us, though we may share the same *ruach* (breath) as we sit together inhaling the same air, though God's universal *ruach* (spirit) sustains each of us, we do not share the same *neshamah*. Your *neshamah* is uniquely yours, different from every other *neshamah* on earth. It is your personalization of God's universal *ruach*. The *neshamah* is God's as well, but we have taken ownership of it in a way we cannot do with *ruach*. Because our *neshamah* distinguishes us from all other people, it is linked to personality, character, and identity in a way that *ruach* is not. What Job understands clearly is that these two essential and inseparable forces within us, forces that seem so very much like our own are in fact not ours, or at least not ours alone. Job is saying that what seems like yours—your breathing, your spirit, your soul—is also, and even more so, God's.

FLUCTUATING SPIRIT WITHIN

Not only are we dependent on God's spirit for life, but Torah also teaches that while we are alive our *ruach* can become stronger or weaker, depleted or more robust in relation to emotions like grief, hope, fear, and despair. In this sense, the *ruach* that is within us corresponds to vigor or vitality and is closely linked to emotion. The life force within us can drain away or become more vital. This is much like we use the word *spirit* in English—"their spirits were flagging" or "it revived his spirit." When a mourning Jacob learns that his favorite son, Joseph, long ago presumed dead, is still alive, Torah records: *"Vatechi ruach Ya'akov avihem—Jacob their father's spirit came to life"* (Gen. 45:27). Many of us can relate to this experience of lost vitality when grieving, and the return of it upon hearing good news.

The Bible uses evocative language to describe the fluctuation of spirit within us. For example, it teaches that fear can affect the strength of our *ruach*. When the kings of the Amorites and Canaanites hear how the Eternal has dried up the waters of the Jordan for the Israelites to cross, "they lost heart and no more *ruach* was left in them." (Josh. 5:1) They lost their fighting spirit, their courage. Our spirits can be troubled, as Pharaoh's is after his disturbing dreams (Gen. 41:8). In deep despair, the psalmist writes, "I cry aloud to God; I cry to God that he may give ear to me. . . . I call to God, I moan, I complain, my spirit fails" (Ps. 77:2,4). Sadness diminishes our spirits. The book of Proverbs teaches: "By sorrow of the heart the spirit is crushed" (15:13). As slaves in Egypt, our spirits were so crushed by cruel bondage that we could not, or would not, listen to words of hope. We could not believe that change was possible. It takes a certain amount of intact spirit to be able to hope for a better future.

Tanakh teaches that God gives us *ruach*, breath and life force, sustains us with it, and it gives us vitality, will, courage, and direction. We call strong-willed children "spirited." This same universal force that we draw on for life and vigor we use to forge our own path, to follow our own inclinations (see Ezek. 13:3). Proverbs advises us to control our spirits (29:11), but when our independent force of spirit goes too far, when we use our vigorous spirit to dominate others, we need to be reined in. The psalmist imagines God placing limits on the dominating spirit of those with power: God "curbs the *ruach* of the princes; inspires awe in the kings of the earth" (Ps. 76:13—which is Ps. 76:12 in most Christian Bibles).

When our emotions are stirred up, our spirits "awaken" (2 Chron. 21:16). When we fear that we have been betrayed, we are overtaken by a spirit of jealousy (Num. 5:14), whereas one who cools his spirit has greater understanding (Prov. 17:27). When we have length of spirit, *erech ruach*, we are patient (Eccles. 7:8). When we are described as short of spirit, we are impatient (Mic. 2:7). When we are depleted, it is as if our spirit has been drained. After three weeks of mourning and fasting, Daniel sees a vision but can barely speak for his emotional and physical exhaustion: "How can this servant of my lord speak with my lord, seeing that my strength has failed and no spirit is left in me?" (Dan. 10:17).

Daniel was given the strength to speak. The Hebrew slaves did gain the strength of spirit to find hope. When our spirits are crushed, the psalmist teaches again and again, God will come to our aid and revive our spirits. Isaiah says of God, "I who make spirits flag, also create the breath of life" (Isa. 57:16). Ultimately, the same one who makes us weak of spirit gives us our breath and our souls and has the power to renew them.

SPEECH SHAPES SPIRIT

From the moment of our first breath of life until the moment of our last, we have within us a fluttering, feeling, fragile spirit. Given the gift of our fluctuating spirit within us, how will we use it? This is Job's test, a test that centers on speech. The *satan* and God want to know: will Job, even in the face of the harshest suffering, ever blaspheme God? The test could have been based on action—would Job continue to make sacrifices to God, to honor God with fair business practices or the care of his body?—but speech holds a special place in Jewish thought.

It is with speech, shaped *ruach*, that God creates the world. Speech has exceptional power to create or to destroy. Job says, "As long as God's spirit is in me, as long as God's breath is in me, my lips shall speak no wrong, nor my tongue utter deceit." (Job 27:3–4) This life breath that enters us and sustains us represents God's faith in us and therefore obligates us to use it well. Job is saying that our lips and tongue, which form that God-given breath into words, should not use *ruach* for deceit or harm. Given our dependence on God's *ruach*, given that our breath is God's gift, we ought to use it only for good.

Careful speech is a focal point of Jewish ethics. Going by the name *lashon hara*, the evil tongue, a large body of teachings acknowledges how tempting it is to use the breath that God gives us to cause harm to others or to speak untruths. Though Jewish tradition emphasizes *teshuvah*, a process of repair and repentance for our harmful acts, many Jewish teachings suggest that the harm of words can never be undone.

In a Hasidic tale, a man goes about the town spreading malicious gossip and then, realizing how much harm he has done, goes to his rabbi to ask for forgiveness and a way to do *teshuvah*, to repair what he had done. The rabbi instructs the man to cut open a feather pillow and walk about the town scattering the feathers in the wind. The man does as he is told. When he returns, the rabbi says, "Now, go gather up every feather. It will be just as difficult as taking back the malicious words that you spread."

The book of Proverbs teaches: "A healing tongue is a tree of life; but a devious one makes for a broken spirit" (15:4). When we use our speech to harm, it is a break with the flow of spirit linking us to God. In verse 26:4, Job asks his friends, who are blaming him for his own suffering, *nishmat-mi yatza mimecha*, "Whose breath came from you?" Take more care with how you use God's breath! God's breath is only to be used to express wisdom and understanding. If you are using breath for another purpose, where did it come from?

Job continues: "Now I open my lips; my tongue forms words in my mouth. My words bespeak the uprightness of my heart; my lips utter insight honestly. The spirit [*ruach*] of God formed me, the breath [*nishmat*] of God sustains me" (Job 33:2–4). Creation and revelation are dancing together—our ongoing creation imposes obligation on how we live. The fact of our dependence on God has implications for how we use our breath, our lips, our tongue. "Therefore, men of understanding, listen to me," Job concludes, "wickedness be far from God, wrongdoing, from Shaddai! . . . If he but intends it, he can call back his spirit [*ruach*] and breath [*neshamah*]; all flesh would at once expire, and humankind return to dust." (Job 34:10, 14–15) None of us knows when this brief wink of a life will be over; none of us knows how many more breaths we have. Let us use them only for good. Let us make ourselves instruments for good with what time we have; let us use each breath to contribute harmony to this glorious interplay of creation.

3
Spirit as a Way to God

A S WE'VE SEEN, HUMAN BEINGS LIVE because we have been given life breath, spirit. Our spirits, which are entwined with our bodies, are God's image within us. We are vulnerable beings, dependent moment to moment on God's spirit for our lives, and through it we are interconnected with the world around us.

Now, what is the experience of having God's spirit within us? What do we feel? What do we yearn for? How can we, as beings holding God's spirit, find God? What do Jewish voices in Tanakh teach us about being human and reaching for transcendence?

BREATH OF PRAISE

In the end, although we may use our spirits for our own purposes, although we may even choose to use our breath to degrade creation, every enspirited thing exists to praise its Creator. If we are wise, we will shape our life breath into speech that elevates, speech that reminds us of the majesty of creation that we are privileged to witness and share. When we do this, and when we pay attention to the feeling and experience of our spirits, we just may find through them a way to God.

The last of the psalms, Psalm 150, declares, *Kol Haneshamah tehallel yah, Halleluyah*. "Every breathing thing, every enspirited thing, uses that spirit/breath to offer words and song of praise. Let all that breathes praise Yah." We exist to stand in awe at the majesty of this blink of existence, and to praise. There is no higher purpose for our life breath than its use in words of love, gratitude, and awe. As Abraham Joshua Heschel says, "The service of prayer, the worship of the heart, fulfills itself not in the employment of words as a human expression, but in the celebration of words as a holy reality. . . . Praying means to take hold of a word, the end, so to speak, of a line that leads to God. . . . But praying also means that the echo of the word falls like a plummet into the depths of the soul."

Heschel continues, "Whose ear has ever heard how all the trees sing to God? Has our reason ever thought of calling upon the sun to praise the Lord? And yet, what the ear fails to perceive, what reason fails to conceive, our prayer makes clear to our souls. It is a higher truth, to be grasped by the spirit: 'All Thy works praise Thee' (Psalm 145:10). We are not alone in our acts of praise. Wherever there is life, there is silent worship. The world is always on the verge of becoming one in adoration." Each of us "is the cantor of the universe, and in whose life the secret of cosmic prayer is disclosed."[20] Though all of life praises God, it is we alone who can form life breath into words, who can express and disclose the secret of cosmic prayer.

TETHERED TO GOD

Because we are a tangle of matter and spirit, we are not just physical but also contain within us a wisp of transcendence. Because the spirit within us is interwoven with our bodies, we can feel our relation to God with our hearts and know it with our minds. We can act on it with our hands, says Hermann Cohen, and this interconnection of the spiritual and the physical in human beings establishes the link between God and each of us.[21]

When, as children or adults, we have a moment of insight—a quivering in the chest, a sense that we belong to something greater than ourselves—we are experiencing spirit inside of us. Again, Cohen says, "God is the Creator, the Molder, of the spirit of man. Hence, spirit relates God to man, and man to God."[22] Cohen goes on to explain that our spirits are not only gifts from God, but they are also our portion or share in God. It is as if each of us is tethered to God by our spirits. Wherever we may roam and whatever we may do, we have a place of belonging in God, a portion that links us always to the Holy One.

Jews often use the word *holiness*, rather than *spirit*, to describe the feeling of connection and belonging to God and the actions that emerge from that relationship. Though both spirit and holiness relate humanity to God, they do so differently. We are born with spirit, but we strive for holiness. Spirit is what we share with God through our creation; holiness is what we aspire to share with God through our actions.

It is possible to live as though the spiritual dimension does not exist, with our attention only on the physical dimension of life. In the physical dimension, we may acknowledge God as Creator, but we do not experience our relation and connection to God. It is only when we live within the spiritual dimension as well as the physical dimension that we become aware of ourselves as more than just matter. That is when we can truly listen for and feel our relationship to God.

SPIRIT WITHIN US AND BEYOND US

As we become aware of ourselves and our world as more than matter, we find ourselves yearning to feel, understand, and listen for God. When constructed as a verb, the root of the word *ruach* (composed of three Hebrew letters, *resh-vav-chet*, or *r-v-ch*) means to become spacious or to feel relieved. Some experience the feeling of connection to God through spirit as a wondrous spaciousness that they hope to repeat again and again. Some feel that they have found relief in the awareness that they are part of an all-encompassing oneness, and they strive to return to that awareness often. Some seek to understand the meaning of their experience, to know more about the spiritual dimension. An inward journey begins.

Where and how do we find God? Given that God's spirit is our starting place within us, we might search for God through our spirits. We have seen that Tanakh is ambiguous about the relation between breath, wind, and spirit, and about the relationship between God's spirit and God. This leaves us with questions: If in some places in Torah it seems that wind is God's breath, might we not look for God in the wind? If our breath and spirit are given and taken together, are breath and spirit one and the same?

Our generation is not the first to seek God. The Tanakh is populated by figures seeking God and searching for understanding of God's will. The Prophet Elijah is one of them. "And lo, the Eternal passed by. There was a great and mighty wind, splitting mountains and shattering rocks by the power of the Eternal; but the Eternal was not in the wind" (1 Kgs. 19:11). Amos reminds us that God created the wind (Amos 4:13), and Jeremiah imagines the wind as God's treasure, residing in God's treasure house until

God calls it forth (Jer. 10:13). The psalmist describes God holding in the wind, releasing it for his purposes (Ps. 135:7), and traveling "on the wings of the wind" (Ps. 104:3). The Tanakh describes the wind doing God's will (Ps. 148:8), whether through storm (Ps. 107:25), the drying of mighty rivers (Isa. 11:15), the calming of the heavens (Job 26:13), or the destruction of empires: "See I am rousing a destructive *ruach* against Babylon" (Jer. 51:1). Wind can enter the smallest crevice (Job 41:16), but human beings cannot control the wind, or hold onto it. Like God, it is ungraspable, beyond us (Eccles. 1:17). It is a sign of our impermanence, particularly in relation to God. "Man, his days are like those of grass; he blooms like a flower of the field; a wind passes by and it is no more, its own place no longer knows it" (Ps. 103:15–16).

As we have noted, it is often unclear when reading Tanakh whether in a given instance the word *ruach* means wind or God's breath. It is not clear whether what we experience as wind might not, in fact, be imagined as God's breath moving through the world. In some cases, Tanakh teaches that the wind comes from God's nostrils (Ps. 18:16). In others the wind is clearly different from breath—when God holds the wind in God's hands or releases it from his treasure house. Elijah makes clear that, though God created the wind and controls it, God is not in the wind.

Though they are closely related, breath and spirit are not one and the same. Our breath keeps us alive, but without spirit, breath makes us only creatures. In fact, breath can be a symbol of our mortality and insignificance. "O, cease to glorify man, who has only a breath in his nostrils! For by what does he merit esteem?" (Isa. 2:22).

In some instances, it seems that God's spirit and God are one and the same. When the psalmist pleads with God, "Do not cast me out of your presence or take your holy spirit away from me!" (51:13), he is expressing a yearning to be near to God, in intimate and unbroken relation with his Creator, but he is also drawing a parallel between God's *ruach hakodesh*, "holy spirit," and God's presence. Perhaps we can relate to this, the feeling that our link to God is fragile and unpredictable, that we may reach for God, for the awareness of spirit and the feeling of connection, and come up empty. Perhaps we have been suffering, feeling alone and despairing, and been unable to feel or remember our belonging and trust in the Holy One.

At one moment fearing God's absence, the psalmist in another moment is aware of God's omnipresence. "Where can I escape from your spirit? Where can I flee from your presence? If I ascend to heaven you are there, if I descend to Sheol you are there too. If I take wing with the dawn to come to rest on the western horizon, even there your hand will be guiding me" (Ps. 139:7–10). Just as we may sometimes feel cut off from God's spirit, at other times we may sense that God's spirit fills the world around us. The psalmist here is linking God's spirit, God's presence, and God's hand. Some may conclude from these parallels that God's spirit is God, but this could just as well be figurative speech. Just as the psalmist is comparing God's hand to God's presence as a figurative way to illustrate God's guiding way, the psalmist may be comparing God's spirit to God's presence to illustrate God's accessibility.

Given that in Judaism God is not embodied and that, according to Elijah, God is not within the forces of nature, some theorize that God is *only* spirit. However, just as there are many nonmaterial forces in the natural world—electromagnetic fields, wind, light, sound—there are many different aspects of the spiritual world. *Neshamah* and *ruach* are different but interrelated. In Torah, angels, God's messengers, are different from God. If we look at the pattern of usage in the Hebrew Bible, we find that God is more than spirit. God's *ruach* is of God and identified with God but not the same as God. God's *ruach* is related to God in a similar way to how our *ruach* is related to our *nefesh chayah*, our living being.

In the following plea from the psalmist, we see the full picture of God's spirit: "Fashion a pure heart for me, O God; create in me a steadfast spirit. Do not cast me out of your presence, or take your holy spirit away from me. Let me again rejoice in your help; let a vigorous spirit sustain me" (Ps. 51:12–14). God creates our spirit within us, a spirit that sustains us with vigor and that can turn us toward God in steadfastness. When we pay attention to our spirit within us, we find ourselves yearning to be in God's presence.

WHEN SPIRIT RETURNS TO GOD

We live in dependence on the spirit of God, which creates the universe, and it is also God's spirit that gives humanity our dignity. Within an individual, God's spirit is like a waxing and waning wind, an ebb and flow of vital energy; but in the world, God's spirit is a continual presence.[23] The spirits of all living things return to God, but God sends forth God's spirit once more and all living creatures are created anew. As Psalm 104 makes clear, God can withdraw *ruach* at any time. Human life is sustained by God's spirit, and one day this spirit will leave us and we will die. In Genesis, God declares that human life is finite: "Adonai said, 'My spirit will not dwell within man forever, since he too is flesh'" (Gen. 6:3).

For some, our days are few, for others many. Some live lives of blessing and comfort, others of great suffering. But God's spirit will not dwell within any of us forever. We know that for each of us a day will come when breath will cease and spirit will leave us. As Job said upon learning of the death of his ten children, "Adonai has given, Adonai has taken away, blessed be the name of Adonai" (Job 1:21).

We see a number of examples in Torah in which God is described as the source of the spirit of all life, and death is described as the removal of that spirit. When, out in the wilderness, Korach and his followers organized a rebellion against Moses and failed, they faced their deaths. Appealing to God as the source of the spirit of all living things, "they fell on their faces and said, 'O God, God of the spirits of all flesh! When one man sins will you be wrathful with the whole community?'" (Num. 16:22). When the flood destroyed all life on dry land, the earth's creatures were described as possessing both breath and spirit of life in their nostrils. "All in whose nostrils was the breath and spirit of life [*nishmat-ruach chayim*], all that was on dry land, died" (Gen. 7:22). God gave the prophet Elijah the ability to return breath/spirit to a child. When Elijah visits the widow of Zarephath, "the son of the mistress of the house fell sick, and his illness grew worse, until he had no breath/spirit [*neshamah*] in him." Elijah called out, "'O Lord my God, let this child's life return to his body!' Adonai heard Elijah's plea, the child's life returned to his body, and he revived" (1 Kgs. 17:17, 21).

God can not only take away and return breath/spirit, but God can also use the divine breath to destroy life, whether at the end of life or in response to evil. "Grass withers, flowers fade when the breath of Adonai blows on them. Indeed man is but grass" (Isa. 40:7). "As I have seen those who plow evil and sow mischief reap them; they perish by a breath from God, are gone at the breath of his nostrils" (Job 4:8–9). When God is particularly full of wrath, such as against the Assyrian Empire, the divine breath can burn like fire. "With plenty of fire and firewood, and with the breath of Adonai burning in it like a stream of sulfur" (Isa. 30:33).

Kohelet, the one who speaks in Ecclesiastes, writing in the last years of his life, is contemplating its meaning and its end. There is not much reason, Kohelet finds, for humanity to chase after *ruach*. We have what we have been given, and ultimately we will all return to where we came from. As he contemplates death, Kohelet observes that no matter how wise we have become, no matter what we have accomplished as human beings, in the end we are much like the beasts of the field. "For in respect of the fate of man and the fate of beast, they have one and the same fate: as the one dies so does the other, and both have the same *ruach*; man has no superiority over beast, since both amount to nothing. Both go to the same place; both came from dust and both return to dust" (Eccles. 3:19–20).

We die in much the same way that the first human being, the *adam*, was formed. We came from dust and we return to dust. Watching this, Kohelet worries that our life breath too may just sink into the earth, no different from beasts. "Who knows if a man's *ruach* does rise upward and if a beast's *ruach* does sink down into the earth?" (Eccles. 3:21).

There is no way to extend or control the day of one's death. "No man has authority over the life breath [*ruach*]—to hold

back the life breath; there is no authority over the day of death"
(Eccles. 8:8). However, when we die, Kohelet concludes, we are
different from beasts, in that our spirits do return to God who
gave them. "The dust returns to the ground as it was, and the life
breath [*ruach*] returns to God who bestowed it" (Eccles. 12:7).
The process of creation is reversed at our deaths. The clay and
dust of our bodies return to the earth, and the life breath, the
spirit within us, returns to God for good.

Judaism does not shy away from death; rather, Judaism emphasizes life. We face the fact that we will die so that we focus
on every fleeting moment of life. From the day that spirit was
first breathed into us to the moment it is taken away, we stand in
the midst of the whirling cosmos that is birthed and breathed by
ruach Elohim. We see that the lush and variegated world we inhabit
is more than matter—it is alive with spirit. Every second of every
day, the symbiotic ecosystem to which we belong is created and
sustained. Each of our own breaths is a reminder. We stand in awe
before this majesty, feeling called to use our breath to sing out
in gratitude and praise, to use our words for good. As we listen
for and feel spirit within us, we reach through it to God, seeking
closeness, understanding, and relationship—seeking revelation.

PART TWO

Revelation: Sinai's Inspiration

4
The Covenant at Sinai

*W*E HAVE SEEN THAT, IN JEWISH TRADITION God's spirit birthed our world and breathes all life into existence. We've learned that Judaism teaches that our spirits and our bodies are not separate but intertwined and that we are profoundly interconnected with life and the world around us through breath and spirit. We've heard the psalmist express a longing to be close to God's spirit, and we have learned that Jewish tradition sees the human spirit as our tether to God, our way to be near.

Because God gave us *ruach*, filled us with breath and spirit, we—all human beings—exist. Because God inspired us with teaching, and endowed us with *ruach* enough to understand, we—the Jewish people—are in covenant. While the story of creation centers on the physical universe, the story of revelation centers on the moral universe. Here we are, each of us, alive for a fleeting moment in the story of our world—looking out at the vast night of stars for a sense of belonging, looking inward to our spirits for a sense of meaning. "Why do I exist?" we ask ourselves. "What is my purpose here?" We stand taking in the splendor of the created world, aware that we live because we breathe, that every living thing is sustained moment by moment by God's spirit. And we want to know what we are meant to do with our lives. We will find that in Jewish tradition God's spirit is not only central to our existence and our relationship with God but also to our awareness and understanding of our purpose while we live.

Exactly fifty days after the Israelites emerge from slavery in Egypt and take our first breaths of desert air as free people, we arrive at Mount Sinai. After we prepare ourselves for three days, God descends on the mountain in cloud. The earth is shaking. The mountain is burning, the smoke rising like that of a kiln. The sound of the shofar (the great horn) is growing louder and louder. There is lightning. There is thunder. Torah teaches that the people, trembling at the base of the mountain alongside their prophet and leader, see voices.

What does it mean that they see voices? Is this a sign of their confusion? Is it a description of a supernatural experience? We do not know. What we do know is that they hear, or see, ten utterances. We call them the Ten Commandments, but the Hebrew literally means ten spoken things. Ten breathed sounds—God's breath forming the sounds of words through fire. The people see no form, no shape, no figure. They stand in awe. Only their own fear prevents them from hearing more. Certain that they cannot survive such intimate encounter with the Source of Life, they call on Moses to serve as intermediary—to hear from God and repeat God's words to the people.

Jewish tradition takes several truths from the account of revelation at Sinai. First, God is beyond the material world and is not physical—we saw no form, shape, or figure. This is the origin of the idea in Jewish tradition that any anthropomorphic or physical description of God is metaphoric. Second, God chose to speak to us collectively, as a people. Every one of the Israelites witnessed God's revelation. In fact, our Midrash teaches that every one of us, in every generation, was there. There's a joke you'll hear Jews make when meeting another Jew for the first time: "I remember you; we stood together in the fifth row back at Sinai!"

Some religious traditions teach that only certain members of the group are fit to be in direct contact with the divine. An important tenet of Judaism is that we are all worthy of, and capable of, direct encounter. Though we had a prophet through whom God could have spoken all revelation, God went to elaborate lengths to speak to us all. If every Jew alive today had a direct encounter with God, this means that somewhere deep within us is the residue of that encounter, a wisp of memory, a feeling. It is our spirit that stirs that latent emotion, giving us the ability to perceive, to witness, to connect once again.

Jewish tradition gleans a third truth from the story of Sinai. At Sinai, revelation was for the purpose of covenant. Revelation was not for the pyrotechnics; rather, God chose to be revealed to us (without form or shape) in order to enter into covenant with us. We, as human beings, are defined by our relationships: none of us exists alone. We are in relationship from the moment of our births and throughout our lives, and it is in the context of relationship that we know ourselves and develop our personalities. The great modern Jewish philosopher Emmanuel Levinas teaches that the nature of our existence is obligation to the Other. Relationship is marked by obligation. From the face of our parents to the face of the stranger, to the face of God, we are throughout our lives

confronted with the demands of the Other. This is the basis of
ethics, Levinas says.

At Sinai, Jewish tradition teaches, we became obligated as a
people. In this singular opportunity for direct communication
with our entire people, God did not give us mystical secrets or a
great deal of information about God, but practical guidance. God
chose to use the moment of revelation to give us *mitzvot*—commandments—specific instructions for how we should live. We
formalized our relationship with God into a covenant, binding
ourselves to God, committing to live our lives in the fulfillment
of God's purpose. Isaiah puts it this way:

> Thus said God Eternal, "Who created the heavens and
> stretched them out, Who spread out the earth and what it
> brings forth, Who gave spirit [*neshamah*] to the people upon
> it, And breath [*ruach*] to those who walk thereon? I, Adonai,
> in my grace have summoned you, and have grasped you
> by the hand. I created you, and appointed you a covenant
> people, a light of nations opening eyes deprived of light,
> rescuing prisoners from confinement, from the dungeon
> those who sit in darkness, I am Adonai, that is my name."
> (Isa. 42:5–8)

The One who stretched out the heavens and spread out the
earth, the One who gave us *neshamah* and *ruach*, has done more
than create us. This God also entered into covenant with the
Jewish people, a covenant based in *mitzvot*, a covenant promising

salvation. In Tanakh, "salvation" refers to collective redemption in this world as opposed to the fate of an individual soul after death.

"Who has plumbed the spirit [*ruach*] of Adonai; What man could tell him His plan?" (Isa. 40:13). According to our people's story of revelation, the Eternal One has a plan for us, a plan that contributes to a destiny for humanity and all of the earth. Isaiah draws a parallel between God's spirit and this plan. It was on Mount Sinai that we first encountered the plan, and it is God's *ruach* that guides us toward fulfillment of that plan. We are unable to see the entire plan, but Jewish tradition teaches that we are to live out this plan through *mitzvot*—specific, prescribed behaviors that repair the world. Thereby, each of us, in our own small way, lives out our purpose, making a contribution to the redemption of our world.

5

Extraordinary Spirit

*I*N ORDER TO UNDERSTAND THE ROLE OF GOD'S SPIRIT in the human capacity to receive revelation, we first look to the examples Jewish tradition gives of extraordinary human beings. We find in Tanakh a handful of individuals said to possess extraordinary spirit. Through their spirits, these people have talents and abilities that enable them to lead or to play a pivotal role in the development of the people and the nation's relationship to God. By looking closely at how Tanakh describes the gifts of these individuals, we can develop a picture of how spirit functions in relation to revelation.

What do people look for in a leader? In addition to the measurable experiences and skills that candidates for public office can demonstrate, we find ourselves drawn to something immeasurable, a certain inspiration or glow. In the language of Torah, those that are particularly inspired possess a heightened measure or quality of *ruach*. We find this in one of the most poignant episodes in all of Torah. Forty years after the inspiring scene at Sinai, as the people are nearing the conclusion of their journey through the wilderness, Moses and God are alone together. God instructs Moses to climb the heights of Mount

Abarim to see the land that he will never enter, the Promised Land. When Moses understands that he will die, his first response is concern not for himself but for the community. How can this wandering people make its way without someone to guide them, to go out before them and come in before them? Moses appeals to Adonai with this appellation: "God of the spirits of all flesh," you who have brought to life and sustains every living thing, you know our limitations. Furthermore, you are invested in these lives, as the source and sustainer of all spirit. You know that without guidance, these people cannot complete your mission and cannot play their unique role in human history. Moses prays: God, appoint someone over this community, someone who shall take them out and bring them in, so that this congregation of the Eternal may not be like sheep that have no shepherd.

God names Moses' successor with these words: "Take to you Joshua, son of Nun, a man that has spirit in him." (Num. 27:18) Given that Moses just called God the source of the spirits of all flesh, their shared understanding is that every living thing has God's spirit in it. So, then, what does it mean that Joshua is a man with spirit in him? Today we would probably call him charismatic, or we might say that he is "inspired"—there is something extraordinary about him related to the quantity or quality of spirit within him. God instructs Moses to lay his hands on Joshua to transfer leadership, and some measure of God's spirit, to him.

Similarly, the prophet Elijah passes a double measure of his spirit to his follower, Elisha, just as he leaves the earth in a fiery chariot. Like Joshua, Elisha is left wearing his mentor's mantle and possessing his spirit. Elisha stands as the inheritor of Elijah's legacy and mission of prophecy on earth like Joshua stands as the inheritor of Moses' legacy and mission of leadership of the Israelite people.

At the very end of Torah, after Moses dies and the people are left in Joshua's command, we read: "Now Joshua son of Nun was filled with the spirit of wisdom because Moses had laid his hands upon him; and the Israelites heeded him, doing as Adonai had commanded Moses" (Deut. 34:9). Not only is he gifted with charisma that inspires his people to follow him, but Joshua also develops wisdom through the *ruach* that is upon him, so that he has the capacity to lead the people in good paths. We will find more about the correlation between spirit and wisdom as we continue our exploration of the role of God's spirit in revelation.

SPIRIT OF DISCERNMENT: LEADERSHIP AND YEARNING

Among the few extraordinary people gifted with a heightened quality or quantity of *ruach*, some are chosen for an even greater measure of *ruach* so that they can lead. This is the case with the first two kings of Israel. When they each become king, Saul and David receive God's spirit upon them. In First Samuel chapter 10, we find Samuel preparing Saul for his journey to become king: "You will encounter a band of prophets coming down from the shrine, preceded by lyres, timbrels, flutes, and harps, and they will be speaking in ecstasy. The spirit of Adonai will grip you, and you will speak in ecstasy along with them; you will become another man. And once these signs have happened to you act when the occasion arises, for God is with you" (1 Sam. 10:5–7). Once God's spirit is resting within Saul, he is transformed and is ready to act as king. "Thereupon the spirit of God gripped him, and he spoke in ecstasy among them" (1 Sam. 10:10).

The Zohar, the foundational work of Kabbalah, composed in thirteenth-century Spain, tells us that Saul was provided with holy spirit when he became king. Different from the Christian idea of Holy Spirit as one of the three Persons of the Trinity, here holy spirit was a "spirit of discernment" that enabled him to judge fairly. According to Rabbi Elliot Gertel, the Zohar saw the holy spirit given to Saul and others as a kind of conduit between individuals and higher levels of divine emanation that gave them access to prophecy. Midrashic and mystical texts compare holy spirit to the Shekhinah, the immanent presence of God featured throughout rabbinic literature.[24] The association between the two manifestations or emanations of God is made in rabbinic commentary on Esther as well, when, in verse 5:1, Queen Esther garbs herself with *malchut*, with her royal garments. The Kabbalists equate *malchut*, one of the ten *sefirot*, or manifestations of the divine, with Shekhinah, and in turn with holy spirit.[25]

But again and again, Saul does not follow God's will and instruction, and he fails. When it becomes clear that Saul can be king no longer, God instructs Samuel to find a different king, a son of Jesse. Samuel invites Jesse and his sons to a sacrificial feast. Jesse brings his eldest, Eliab, forward, and Samuel thinks from his height and stature that this is the one. But Adonai says to Samuel, "Pay no attention to his appearance or his stature, for I have rejected him. For not as a man sees [does Adonai see], man sees only what is visible, but Adonai sees into the heart." Jesse brings forward his next son, Abinadab, but he was not the chosen one either, and then Shammah, and then four more sons—but none are right until David comes forward. Adonai says to Samuel, "Rise and anoint him for this is the one." And then the Tanakh reports, "Samuel took the horn of oil and anointed him in the presence of his brothers; and the spirit of Adonai gripped David from that day on" (1 Sam. 16:7–13).

David's gift of holy spirit is regarded as qualitatively different from Saul's by both Midrash and the Zohar, because David actively sought and praised God. According to the Zohar, which again equates holy spirit with the Shekhinah, it was David's yearning for holy spirit that caused it to rest on him.[26] Holy spirit either remains with David or visits him repeatedly, giving him revelations concerning the future of Israel.[27] These stories of Saul and David teach that receiving God's spirit is more than a passive affair, that one's yearning for spirit and praise of God enables God's spirit to remain and return.

Here we see extraordinary leaders, individuals chosen by God to receive God's spirit. In the cases of Joshua and Elisha, receiving God's spirit enabled them to take on the mantle of their predecessors and lead. In the cases of Saul and David, Jewish tradition sees the holy spirit as a kind of conduit between the receiver and God, enabling the person to see and understand God's will more clearly. The Shekhinah, the indwelling presence of God, which Jewish tradition teaches accompanies us when we study Torah or gather in community, is present for extraordinary leaders to help guide them in their judgments. But, contrasting the cases of Saul and David, we learn that being chosen is not enough. One must live up to the bestowed spirit in at least two ways: by following its guidance and reaching out for God. The Midrash teaches that because

David praised and yearned for God, the holy spirit returned to him again and again.

Though we are not like Saul and David, perhaps we can relate to their experience. Those who develop a spiritual practice, whether through meditation or prayer, often find that regularly feeling for God's presence and expressing gratitude for the blessings of life makes a difference. By reaching out and turning toward God's presence, we can awaken our sense of spirit within us and feel that we are not alone.

SPIRIT OF REVELATION: WISDOM, UNDERSTANDING, AND KNOWLEDGE

What is this gift of *ruach* among extraordinary people that we see in Joshua, Elisha, Saul, and David? How does it manifest itself? Descriptions of Bezalel, Hiram, and the *mashiach* may give us additional clues.

Back at Mount Sinai, long before Moses' transmission of leadership to Joshua, it was time to build the Tabernacle, the portable sanctuary for ongoing encounter between God and the Israelites. Here the people would offer their sacrifices (in Hebrew *korbanot*, from the root *k-r-b*, meaning "drawing near"). The Tabernacle would be the place where the people could reach for God, and where God would descend in the form of a cloud to dwell among the people. This led, generations later, to the concept of the Shekhinah, the aspect of God that dwells among us like the cloud of Presence within the Tabernacle. The Zohar calls the Shekhinah the "Spirit of Holiness" drawing down divine emanation from the higher realms to the earthly plane.[28]

God dictated precise instructions for the construction of the Tabernacle. But who could be trusted to create this portal between the realms of human and divine? An artisan of great talents was singled out for the task: Bezalel. For, as God declares, Bezalel possesses the gift of *ruach*. "I have endowed him with a divine *ruach* of *chochmah*, *binah*, and *da'at* in every kind of craft" (Exod. 31:3). The Hebrew words used for Bezalel's gift of *ruach*— *chochmah*, *bina*, and *da'at*—are not only associated with this one man. They appear together three times in Tanakh to describe God's *ruach* resting on extraordinary human beings. These are the three words that describe the artisan chosen for the metalwork of the Holy Temple: "King Solomon sent for Hiram and brought him down from Tyre. . . . He was endowed with *chochmah*, *tevunah* [from the same root as *bina*], and *da'at* for executing all work in bronze. He came to King Solomon and executed all his work" (1 Kgs. 7:13–14).

These same three words are used to describe the gift of an awaited leader: "*Ruach* Adonai will rest upon him; a spirit of wisdom and insight [*ruach chochmah u'vinah*], a spirit of counsel and valor, a spirit of knowledge [*da'at*] and awe for Adonai" (Isa. 11:2). These gifts will enable him to rule with justice and righteousness (Isa. 11:4). And these words also describe God's work of creating the world: "Adonai founded the earth by *chochmah*, established the heavens by *tevunah*; by Adonai's *da'at* the depths burst apart, and the skies distilled dew" (Prov. 3:19–20).

What are these three attributes of spirit that enable God to create the world, Bezalel to create the Holy Tabernacle, and Hiram to create the metalwork for the Holy Temple? How are these the same qualities that the ideal human leader (later identified as the *mashiach,* messiah) will have to lead our world toward peace and justice? *Chochmah, tevunah,* and *da'at* are translated variously as skill, ability, and talent; wisdom, understanding, and knowledge; and knowledge, insight, and devotion. A Hebrew dictionary would give us the second set of definitions: *chochmah* is wisdom; *tevunah* is understanding; *da'at* is knowledge. But even in English, do we quite know what we mean by these three concepts and how they differ from each other?

That greatest rabbinic commentator in history, Rashi, commenting on the verses about Bezalel, defines these three words as follows: "*chochmah*: what a person learns from others; *tevunah*: understanding things from his heart, from the things he has learned; *da'at*: the holy spirit [*ruach hakodesh*]." When we think of wisdom, we tend to think of an internal quality that develops with age, a quality that may lead one to see things quite differently than the people around her. But isn't wisdom the ability to always learn from others? Doesn't it develop with age, because through life experience we accumulate lessons from others? This is Rashi's definition of wisdom.

Moses Mendelssohn, writing a commentary called the *Biur* in the eighteenth century, adapts Rashi's definition of *chochmah*. He sees wisdom as the ability to know the means to the end: "A knowledge of the technique by which we achieve our desires is termed *chochmah*," Mendelssohn says. A wise person, he continues, is "one who understands how to achieve the genuine good."[29] In this way, when we describe a person as wise, we mean that he knows how to live a good life.

So, the first element that *ruach* gives extraordinary people is the ability to learn from others to discern how to live a good life. What is the second element? How is understanding different from wisdom?

Rashi says that an understanding person is one who is able to integrate the life lessons of wisdom, internalize them in his heart, and apply them to new situations. Mendelssohn describes *tevunah* as follows: *"Tevunah* refers to the ability to deduce one thing from another and achieve the unknown from the known." Therefore, *tevunah* is about bridge building, making links between what is already known and what is not yet known, using the known to elucidate the unknown. But *tevunah* is also its opposite. Mendelssohn says: "The root [of *tevunah*] is *bein* ["between"] since one who can differentiate between things is capable of intellectual achievements."[30] In other words, *tevunah* is about both making associations and making distinctions. Seeing how two dissimilar things are related and seeing how two related things are dissimilar are both part of understanding.

Now we know that *ruach* gives extraordinary people the ability to learn from others and awareness about how to live a good life, as well as the ability to integrate and apply that wisdom in making connections and distinctions. We can see that these would be very powerful qualities to enable a person to receive revelation about God's purpose in the world. A person who is always able to learn from others can move beyond fixed concepts and expectations—beyond what he thinks he already knows. A person who can apply those insights to see the diversity and interconnections among everything that exists is moving beyond the limited perspective of a single human being. Stepping back to see the world from a transcendent perspective, this person can then apply that perspective to gain clarity about how to live a good life. We would certainly call a person like this wise and understanding. We may also feel that such a person has extraordinary spirit, such that he or she seems particularly aware in his or her relationship to God.

It is Rashi's third definition that has raised questions throughout the ages. Remember, these three words—*chochmah*, *tevunah*, and *da'at*—are the three defining characteristics of *ruach*, God's spirit given to extraordinary people to enable them to create or lead. Rashi defines *da'at*, the third element that constitutes the gift of *ruach*, as *ruach hakodesh*, the holy spirit. What does Rashi, known for precise language, mean by defining *ruach* with the word *ruach*?

Rabbi Yitzhak Elhanan Spektor, who lived in Russia in the nineteenth century, wrote a commentary called *Be'er Yitzchak* (the *Well of Yitzchak*) in 1858. In it he elucidates Rashi's interpretation of these three capacities afforded to us through God's spirit. To explain Rashi's association of *da'at* with holy spirit, Spektor asks us to examine the Hebrew verb form of *yada* ("know") from which *da'at* is formed, showing that it "connotes the spiritual kinship engendered by the coming together of two forces. 'Adam knew [*yada*] Eve his wife'—connotes the feeling of intimacy between them. . . . Any intense feeling, whether of pleasure or pain, caused by . . . close contact . . . with something external is expressed by the verb *yada* (sensing or knowing). In other words, we can express the perceptiveness and wisdom engendered in man's soul through its contact with the divine by the word *da'at*."[31]

According to Spektor, *da'at* is not knowledge as we usually use the term in English: to mean facts or information acquired through reading or experience. Spektor says that knowledge is deeply intimate relation with another. That is why the same verb root is used to describe sexual relations. In this case, *da'at* is describing an intimate relationship between a human being and God. This intimate relationship is made possible by an extra measure of *ruach*, God's holy spirit, which God bestows on the individual. This capacity to know God enables the person to create or lead as if the creation is coming through them.

Many artists describe the experience of an artwork emerging whole, or creative ideas flowing through them as if the inspiration came from a source outside of themselves. The great American choreographer and dancer Martha Graham said,

> There is a vitality, a life force, a quickening that is translated through you into action, and there is only one of you in all time, this expression is unique, and if you block it, it will never exist through any other medium; and be lost. The world will not have it. It is not your business to determine how good it is, nor how it compares with other expression. It is your business to keep it yours clearly and directly, to keep the channel open. You do not even have to believe in yourself or your work. You have to keep open and aware directly to the urges that motivate you.[32]

This is *da'at*. This is what it feels like to have *ruach hakodesh*, God's holy spirit, rest within you.

Mendelssohn's definition of *da'at* expands on Rashi's. "*Da'at* refers to the ability to perceive forms as they are whether they are sensory or extra-sensory."[33] In other words, there are forms ready to be created. Some we can see or hear or feel and imitate. Others are nowhere to be found with our senses but exist nonetheless, and they are waiting for us to bring them into the world. Those with *da'at* are able to perceive those forms, to listen for them, to see them in their mind's eye and create them in the world. They are able to do this, Rashi would say, because they are in intimate contact with the Holy One and because they have an extra measure of God's *ruach* bestowed on them.

These texts about Bezalel, Hiram, and the ideal human leader, or *mashiach* teach us that it is through God's *ruach* that meaning is revealed. Through an intimacy with God's spirit, these extraordinary people are able to discern how to live a good life, to see the connections between disparate phenomena (the one within the many), and to feel and envision fully formed creations. They thus possess a high moral sensibility, an intuitive and integrative capacity, and creative genius: three qualities that make them powerful leaders and visionaries. These qualities enable a person to serve as a conduit for God's revelation in the world and to bring about transformation. According to Jewish tradition, these are some, but not all, of the gifts that come when God's spirit rests on extraordinary human beings. There are more.

SPIRIT OF COURAGE: RISING TO SAVE OTHERS

God's *ruach* is not only what sustains us, and not only what gives us insight and understanding. It is not only what provides for extraordinary leadership and prophecy. It can also descend on some of us, grip us, and enable us to do amazing things.

On the morning of December 19 of 2009 in Ottawa, Kansas, a man named Nick Harris was dropping his daughter off at school when he saw a car back over a six-year-old girl. "I didn't even think," he said. "I ran over there as fast as I could, grabbed the rear end of the car and lifted and pushed as hard as I could." In a flash, the five-foot-seven-inch, 185-pound man found the strength to lift the car off of the child. The girl, Ashlyn Hough, wasn't under the car long enough to be seriously hurt. Other than a concussion and some scrapes, she came away from the incident unharmed. "Somehow, adrenaline, hand of God, whatever you want to call it, I don't know how I did it," Harris said. He went around later that day trying to move or lift other cars and couldn't.[34]

In another incident that year, Lieutenant John Shepherd, a firefighter of the Akron, Ohio, fire department, came to the scene of a car accident where the driver was trapped inside of a burning vehicle. Shepherd climbed into the car and used his body—covered in protective fire gear—to shield the driver from the fire and heat while they waited for the rescue equipment to arrive.[35]

Every year stories like these hit the press, stories of people summoning extraordinary courage and strength in a moment of crisis. These stories lead us to ask ourselves, what would I do? Would I have the courage to sacrifice myself in this way? Would I be able to lift a car off of a child? What is it that descends on people that endows them with physical strength and bravery?

In his *Guide for the Perplexed*, Moses Maimonides ranks eleven levels of prophecy found in Scripture. The first two levels on the scale are encounters with God's *ruach*, which he notes are not quite prophecy but the foundations of prophecy. In the first level of Maimonides' schema, a person is inspired to perform some great, altruistic act with a sudden display of extraordinary courage and strength. Maimonides says:

To deliver a congregation of good men from the hands of evil doers . . . the individual himself is prompted to the deed. This degree of Divine influence is called "the spirit of the Lord." Of such a person we say that the spirit of the Lord came upon him, or rested upon him, or that the Lord was with him, etc. This was the case with the judges of Israel (Judges 11:29, 14:19; Samuel 11:6, Chronicles 12:19). Moses too was always distinguished by this prophetic spirit. It prompted him to slay the Egyptian, to prevent injustice between the two men who quarreled, and at Midian, at the well. Whenever he saw wrong being done, he could not restrain himself, as it is said, "And Moses rose and saved them" (Exodus 2:17).[36]

As we saw, the spirit of God rested on Saul from the moment of his anointing, priming him for acts of great courage and leadership. When Nahash the Ammonite marches against the people of Jabesh-gilead, commanding them to gouge out their right eye in an act of submission and humiliation, the people all across Israel break out in weeping. When he heard this, Tanakh reports that once again, "the spirit of God gripped Saul." Now three layers of God's spirit are on Saul: the measure of spirit given to every human being, the additional gift he received when anointed and in a state of ecstasy, and this measure that came upon him in an emergency, in a time of great need. This third measure causes Saul's anger to blaze up, leading him to muster an army of 330,000 to save the men of Jabesh-gilead (1 Sam. 11:6).

In the book of Judges, Gideon musters courage from an extra measure of God's spirit: "The spirit of Adonai enveloped [literally, "dressed"] Gideon; he sounded the horn, and the Abiezrites rallied behind him" (Judg. 6:34). Samson is frequently gripped by God's spirit, granting him extraordinary courage and strength: "The spirit of Adonai first moved him in the encampment of Dan, between Zorah and Eshtaol" (Judg. 13:25). Then, when Samson sees a lion, "the spirit of Adonai gripped him, and he tore him asunder with his bare hands as one might tear a kid asunder" (Judg. 14:6). "The spirit of Adonai gripped him. He went down to Ashkelon and killed thirty of its men" (Judg. 14:19). And "the spirit of Adonai gripped him and the ropes on his arms became like flax that catches fire; the bonds melted off his hands" (Judg. 15:14).

In Maimonides' view, reports like these do not mean that God reaches down and puts God's spirit on the altruistic or brave person. Rather, it means that God, whose emanations fill the universe, creates a natural system on earth that includes highly developed courage in some people who are at the ready for a moment of need. And then, in the emergency, there is an overflow of the effluence from God on that person, which inspires him or her to act with strength and resolve.

SPIRIT OF ELOQUENCE: WISDOM OF WORDS

Some find the gift of God's spirit moving through their bodies, giving them strength and courage to do what must be done. Others find the gift of God's spirit moving through their hearts and mouths, enabling them to use words to inspire.

It was said of the Baal Shem Tov, the seventeenth-century founder of Hasidic Judaism in Poland, that when he would speak to a group of his disciples, every one of them would emerge from the evening's lesson certain that the great rabbi had focused his wise and insightful talk only on him, ignoring all of the others. Self-conscious about all of the attention, his listeners would emerge apologetic to their fellow men. To their surprise and confusion, they'd find that all of the others were certain of the same thing.

How do we explain those moments when someone speaks with such eloquence that our breath catches, we are captivated, and the room becomes extraordinarily still? There is electricity between us, a transcendence, as if time is frozen, as if we ourselves are frozen into a single entity, unified by the speaking and the listening. What has come upon us?

In the second level of Maimonides' system, a person has extraordinary intuition, feeling as if something has descended on him or her, giving just the right words, the ability to speak words of wisdom, to captivate and to communicate truth. This is *ruach hakodesh*, the holy spirit of God, a force that arises within a person to write or utter wisdom as if it came from beyond them, through them; and we know when we hear it that it is something extraordinary.

Tradition teaches that it was through the holy spirit of God that David composed the Psalms, and Solomon composed Proverbs, Ecclesiastes, and Song of Songs. "These are the last words of David. . . . The spirit of Adonai has spoken through me, his message is upon my tongue" (2 Sam. 23:1–2). In the Talmud, the sages say, "The scroll of Esther was dictated through the holy spirit" (Babylonian Talmud *Megillah* 7a). According to Maimonides, the holy spirit or intuitive force suddenly appears at some point in a person's life history. It is not something he or she possesses from the beginning of life. It comes only sporadically and then departs. According to Isaac Abrabanel, a Portuguese Jewish statesman, philosopher, and Bible commentator of the fifteenth century, "When a person feels within himself that it is something new, as if from outside, which arises in him . . . it is said that the holy spirit rests upon him."[37]

It is not necessary, Maimonides says, to be extraordinary throughout one's life in order for the holy spirit to descend on a person at a particular moment in time. This raises the possibility that any person may suddenly find within herself great courage or great eloquence, particularly if one develops these qualities over time.

Jewish tradition claims that God is speaking to us all of the time. According to Midrash, the moment at Sinai has never ended. God's voice continues to echo through the world, and it is up to us to listen for how we should live. Sometimes an extraordinary person comes along who is particularly able to hear. Joshua, Elisha, Saul, David, Bezalel, Hiram, the yet-to-be *mashiach*, Gideon, Samson, the Baal Shem Tov, and countless other individuals past and present all share this ability to differing degrees. Each has access to God's spirit in extraordinary measure, attuning him or her to God's voice. For some, like Joshua, this spirit enabled them to lead a people with charisma and wisdom. At best, these leaders strengthened the already-heightened levels of spirit within them by humbling themselves to actively seek out God's voice, by earnestly searching for the right way to live and lead.

Others became conduits for God's creation through their gifts of spirit manifested as wisdom, understanding, and intimacy with God. The secret of the artists, like Bezalel and Hiram, is their ability to feel and see God's creation moving through them, coming out whole. Their wisdom and understanding, like that of the *mashiach* yet-to-come, is their ability to learn from every person, to internalize what they learn in their hearts, to see the underlying connections in the world, and to apply all of this to living a good life.

Maimonides teaches us that countless people have access through spirit to the first two levels of prophecy, by which they are able to act with great courage or speak with gripping eloquence. Unlike Gideon, Samson, and the Baal Shem Tov, who had these gifts throughout their lives, these people whose names we do not know may suddenly find themselves able to act or speak to do what must be done in a moment of need. We learn, too, that these individuals can nurture the gift of spirit they find within themselves, developing their reservoir of courage and their talent at moving an audience with their words. And so, we move from the extraordinary to the ordinary, from a select few named leaders in Tanakh, chosen by God to receive God's spirit, to an unknown set of potential actors who may unexpectedly find themselves enabled by God's spirit to use their bodies and minds to make a difference in the world.

6
Ordinary Spirit

*I*NSPIRING LEADERSHIP, BOLD ACTS OF COURAGE, SUBLIME artistry, profound wisdom, passionate eloquence: Judaism teaches that these are all gifts of God's spirit, each a means for bringing God's revelation into the world. But what about the rest of us, who may or may not display any of these gifts in extraordinary measure?

If God designed revelation at Sinai to speak to every one of us, and if God is continually speaking, continually beckoning to us so that we may understand our purpose in the world, why would the ability to receive revelation through God's spirit be limited to a handful of extraordinary individuals? Surely there must be a way for every person to listen, to receive God's revelation through God's spirit. We find, in Torah, that there is.

RUACH FOR ALL: SHARING THE SPIRIT

An interesting episode occurs at a particular low point in Israel's journey in the wilderness. The people have just set out on their journey from Mount Sinai into the wilderness when they begin to complain bitterly, day in and day out. They are tired of manna; they are tired of wandering. They want meat; they want onions and cucumbers like they had in Egypt. They are fed up with the same old food every day. They are whining; they are threatening revolt. Hearing this, Moses has had enough. He is done. He is tired of being alone as a prophet among Israel, the one leader to whom all turn in their dissatisfaction and need. Moses cries out to God that he neither conceived nor birthed this people and that he "cannot carry all this people by myself, for it is too much for me" (Num. 11:14).

God responds that Moses should identify seventy of Israel's elders whom Moses has experienced as leaders among the people—people tried and true—and bring them together at the Tent of Meeting. These elders are going to take their place with Moses as leaders of the Israelite people. God says, "I will come down and speak with you there, and I will draw upon the spirit that is on you and put it upon them; they shall share the burden of the people with you, and you shall not bear it alone" (Num. 11:17).

We learn from this that God's spirit is not finite. It need not be limited to only one or two special people. Spirit can be shared with all those who are needed to lead, be wise, create, or be brave. Moses' dose of *ruach Elohim* enables him to have one-on-one time with God on a daily basis. God's spirit resting on him gives him the capacity to listen for God's voice and to communicate directly with God. The measure of spirit that is already on Moses can be shared with seventy more, and Moses' leadership abilities are in no way diminished by this distribution. God's spirit is infinite and defies both our ability to quantify and our inclination to limit.

Moses does as he is told. He chooses seventy elders with whom to share the burden of leadership, and he brings them around the

Tent of Meeting. God "drew upon the spirit that was on him and put it upon the seventy elders. And when the spirit rested upon them, they prophesied, but did not continue."

This story would be enough to make our point if it ended here, but it does not. A very curious thing happens. There are two men, Eldad and Medad, men who "were recorded" but remain in the camp and do not join the others around the Tent of Meeting. The spirit rests on these two men and they prophesy in the camp. A young man runs to tell Moses. Joshua becomes concerned: who do these men think they are, acting the part of prophet? Moses responds: "Would that all of Adonai's people were prophets, that Adonai put his spirit upon them!"

The Talmud digs for an explanation. What does it mean that Eldad and Medad were recorded but remained in the camp? One idea presented is that Eldad and Medad were left at the ballot boxes. When Moses was instructed to gather seventy men, he had a dilemma. He needed to treat all twelve tribes equally in order to prevent enmity among the tribes. If he chose six from each tribe, though, the total would be seventy-two, not seventy. So he made seventy slips of paper with the word "elder" and two blank slips. Eldad and Medad chose the two blank slips. They had been recorded but remained in the camp.

But, the Talmud continues, Rabbi Shimon disagrees with this explanation. He says that when Moses included them among the seventy, Eldad and Medad responded, "We are not worthy of this honor." The Holy One said, "Since you belittle yourselves, behold I shall add honor unto your honor." What was the honor that God bestowed on Eldad and Medad? "That all the prophets prophesied but did so no more, while they prophesied but did not cease" (Talmud *Sanhedrin* 17a).

Isaac Abrabanel, writing in the fifteenth century, meshes these two interpretations together: Eldad and Medad were chosen among the seventy-two and, in their great humility and in order to prevent shame from coming to the two who were not chosen, remained of their own free will in the camp.

Why, if they had such merit and were being rewarded, would a leader such as Joshua want to stop them from prophesying? A modern Torah commentator, Nehama Leibowitz, contends that Joshua was concerned about misuse of authority. He thought, she says, "that their inspired volubility smacked of prophetic license. Only those around the Tent of Meeting on whom Moses would bestow his spirit were authorized to prophesy."[38]

Human beings can be competitive with one another. As children on the sports field, we want to be the fastest, to throw the hardest, to hit the most home runs. In school, we want to be the smartest or the most popular. These inclinations live within adults as well. If we find that we have an extra measure of *ruach* in us, a gift or talent, we privately enjoy the ways in which we are exceptional. What happens when our fellow athletes or students are equally gifted? Do we rejoice or do we quietly regret the loss of our advantage? And how often do we feel diminished by the grandeur of others? How often do we shrink for fear that if we shine, others will resent it?

Though Joshua was jealous on Moses' behalf, Moses himself was not at all concerned. When we are at our best, we are not protective of our talents. We know that the world would be a better place if every person could be an instrument of God's will.

We know that we need fully realized human beings to bring about the messianic age.

What happens in this story is most instructive. Moses, who for decades has stood alone as Israel's leader, as the only one with an intimate relationship with God, complains about being the lonely gifted one. He is then given company. This is a test, for most of us would experience a twinge of jealousy, of loss. Moses has lost his uniqueness. By the fact that prophecy is now shared, Moses is a lot more like everyone else.

But Moses is not jealous. He wishes not only that this gift would be shared with every member of the people Israel but also that it be a lasting gift. Martin Buber has us notice Moses' words. Moses does not say, "Would it be that all Adonai's people prophesy." He says, "Would that all Adonai's people were prophets." His ideal would be to have company not just on one rare day but to have his gift shared equally among all of the people forever.[39] Moses envisions a world in which all of the people would be in direct communication with God, receiving divine order directly. If all people could hear God's will directly, the messianic age would arrive. As the prophet Joel proclaims,

> I will pour out My spirit on all flesh;
>
> Your sons and daughters shall prophesy;
>
> Your old men shall dream dreams,
>
> Your young men shall see visions. (Joel 3:1)

Rabbi Samson Raphael Hirsch of the nineteenth century observes: "We are shown that there is no monopoly of spiritual leadership. The spiritual powers granted by God are not the privilege of any particular office or status. The lowliest of the nation shares with the highest the opportunity of being granted Divine inspiration."[40]

SPIRIT OF UNDERSTANDING: A GIFT FOR ALL HUMANKIND

We might have thought that when Moses' spirit was shared with the seventy elders, its strength would dissipate as it spread, like heat or light becomes weaker the farther it radiates from its source. But we have learned that the extraordinary gift of spirit is not limited to a small handful of leaders but is available to at least seventy people in a generation. This raises the question: what about the rest of us?

In our earlier section on creation, we saw that Job attributed his breath and life to God's spirit. Job also sees that the human capacity for insight and awareness comes from God's spirit. "But truly it is the spirit in man, the spirit of God that gives them understanding" (Job 32:8). If, as Job says, it is our God-given spirit that gives us the capacity to understand, God's *ruach* necessarily rests on all of us, enabling us to take in revelation. How then can *ruach* be something given only to those extraordinary individuals who build sanctuaries, lead nations, hear prophecies, and bring about a perfected world?

Abraham Joshua Heschel teaches that "the word 'spirit' in the Bible has more than one meaning. Of Bezalel it is said that he is filled with the spirit of God. . . . Of the prophets we hear that the spirit of God comes upon them. (Isaiah 61:1 Ezekiel 11:5) Of the Messiah we are told that 'the spirit of God shall rest upon him. . . .' (Isaiah 11:2) The spirit in these passages denotes an endowment of chosen men. But, as we have seen, it is also an endowment of all men, it is that which gives them understanding."[41]

Heschel sees two distinct uses of the word *ruach* in the Hebrew Bible—first, something every one of us has, given to us by God, that enables us to understand the spiritual aspects of our world, to perceive and integrate the sublime; and second, a gift to extraordinary people, perhaps an extra measure of *ruach*, that enables them to serve God in extraordinary ways through wisdom, understanding, and knowledge. In other words, though some human beings have an extra measure of *ruach*, God's spirit rests on or within every one of us, enabling us to receive revelation. It is our spirit, God's spirit within us, that allows us to feel for God's will, to understand how we ought to live.

SPIRIT OF AWARENESS: MIRACLES OF EVERYDAY LIFE

Rabbi Lawrence Kushner tells a story in his book *Jewish Spirituality: A Brief Introduction for Christians*, based in the Midrash, of two ordinary guys named Reuven and Shimon. Reuven and Shimon were two of the 600,000 people who escaped from slavery in the great Exodus from Egypt. As they crossed the split sea among the vast multitudes, a wall of water on their left and their right, Pharaoh's army behind, and freedom in the distance, Reuven and Shimon were looking down. "This is terrible!" said Reuven, "There's mud all over the place!" "Disgusting!" said Shimon. "I'm in muck up to my ankles!" All along the walk from slavery to freedom, they continued like this. All through the great miracle of liberation, Reuven and Shimon were looking down, complaining about the mud.[42] Rabbi Kushner teaches that if Reuven and Shimon could fail to notice the splitting of the Red Sea even as they were walking through it, then we can easily fail to notice the smaller miracles of everyday life. If they could be focused on the mud while the sea water stood as walls above them, then we can be focused on the mundane while the holy is on display all around us.

Albert Einstein famously said, "There are only two ways to live your life: as if nothing is a miracle, or as if everything is a miracle." Most days we do live as if nothing is a miracle—the table before me is only a table. A table, what an ordinary thing! Even if we know now that more than 99 percent of that table is black space, that its solidity is an illusion created by whirling electrons so small and moving at such speed that we cannot see the emptiness about which they circle, most days a table does not seem like a miracle.

When we listen, it is God's spirit within us that attunes us to the wonder of life, enables us to perceive the brief winks of God's revelation to us. We are surrounded by miracles in our daily lives, sights and sounds that infants are awed by, toddlers curious about, young children delighted by. We, however, forget to be amazed. Take any simple object—a nickel, for example. Fascinating to children, shiny, smooth metal, mined from deep in the earth; melted, molded with Thomas Jefferson's profile and the words "In God We Trust"; traveling through thousands of hands to reach ours: we could choose to see a simple nickel as worthy of delight. But most of us have, through the habit and routine of daily life, the buying and selling and mechanics of it all, become inured to the wonder of a nickel.

This is the question of revelation. What can we see at any given moment? How do we remember to notice the miracle? Before we knew of atomic structure, there was no way we could see more than a table. Now we know better, but most of us still forget about the miracle of our tables most of the time.

SPIRIT OF SENSITIVITY: LISTENING FOR GOD'S VOICE

It is one thing for God to speak to us, to reach out to us, to give us opportunities for wonder at the top of a mountain or in everyday life. It is quite another for us to hear God, to perceive the miracle, to attune ourselves to God's whispers.

"It is a spirit in man, the spirit of the Almighty that gives them understanding" (Job 32:8). God's *ruach* that hovered over the waters in the first moments of creation is not only the ebb and flow of our physical existence but also the medium of our moral existence. This breath/wind/spirit that we experience dwelling within us is none other than the spirit of God, designed both to keep us alive and to give us meaning. There is a partnership in action between the God-given spirit within us and the spirit of God outside of us working together to give us the sensitivity to perceive the holy and the insight to translate our perceptions into understanding.

This was the case even with the miracle of the burning bush. When Moses stood to behold the burning bush, it was a miracle. But what, exactly, was the miracle? According to Rabbi Kushner, the miracle of the burning bush was not in the fire, or in the bush, or in the fact that the fire did not consume the bush. The miracle at the burning bush was that Moses stopped and turned aside to notice.[43] Only after he stopped, turned aside, and watched for some time did the supernatural phenomenon become apparent. The supernatural phenomenon was not that the bush was aflame (in the scorching heat of the desert this was not so unusual); it was that the fire was not consuming the bush: "yet the bush was not consumed" (Exod. 3:2).

In *Eyes Remade for Wonder*, Kushner asks how long one would need to stop and watch to observe that a fire is not consuming a bush. Only a person attuned to wonder would have the patience to pay such close attention; only those who walk through the world with great sensitivity. Kushner thinks that God was testing Moses here to see if he had the sensitivity needed to be God's prophet, to lead the people out of slavery.

For most of us, a table is where we put dinner, and a burning bush is a reason to call 911. But even the most prosaic among us have our moments, moments when we sense that God's spirit is there. We can feel it sometimes as a rush to the heart, or a sudden sense of belonging. Maybe you have found yourself standing on a mountain, or in the chill of forest, and you thought—this is not an accident. It's too grand to be an accident. You feel, you know, there's something there. Maybe a beloved one died, and you fell and fell, and then you landed. And it was soft and it held you, and you knew that you would live again. These moments, Torah tells us, come to us courtesy of God's *ruach* resting on us, God's gift of spirit that enables us to understand.

SPIRIT OF INSIGHT: SEEING BEYOND EXPECTATION

God's *ruach* not only enables us to see miracles in everyday life, but it also enables us to see beyond our expectations. Our expectations can sometimes limit us. Psychologists have discovered that our expectations influence outcomes—if we expect that there is nothing extraordinary to see, we will see nothing extraordinary. If we expect to fail, we are likely to fail. If we expect to dislike another culture or group, we probably will. If we expect another group to be dangerous or frightening, we are likely to be intimidated in their presence. But in the stories of Balaam and Caleb, we see that *ruach* can help its bearer to see beyond his expectations through a sudden moment of understanding, a different insight.

Balaam was a prophet hired by Balak, a Moabite king, to curse the people Israel into oblivion. Balaam travels to meet the Israelite tribes where they are encamped on the plains of Moab and inflict his curses on them. But before he can curse them, he does something else: he sees them. "As Balaam looked up and saw Israel encamped tribe by tribe, the spirit of God came upon him" (Num. 24:2). The Zohar imagines the spirit of God as one that spreads over the people Israel, as a scarf is spread over the head of a child.[44]

Israel was the object of Balaam's mission, not its subject. Given his mission, it was an object that must be removed, a force that must be stopped. To curse another people, one cannot see them, take in their humanity, their beauty, their *tselem Elohim* (the ways that they are in the divine image). This is what we mean when we talk about viewing others not as human beings but as "the Other." Balaam came with that mission, but *ruach Elohim*, the spirit of God, came upon him. What did he do? "He looked up and saw [them]."

Martin Buber describes this experience of genuinely seeing the other as an I-Thou encounter. Every day in order to function, Buber says, we see others as an It. We see others in terms of their function in our lives—the person checking our food at the supermarket, driving the garbage truck, in front of us in traffic. Now and then, with the help of *ruach Elohim*, we see another as a whole and holy being. We encounter that person instead as a Thou. We draw in our breath at the majesty of this holy being created by God. In Leviticus 19, we are commanded to become holy, for God is holy. My teacher, Rabbi Richard Levy, suggests that we should view every person as though they have the words *kodesh l'Adonai* on their foreheads. *Kodesh l'Adonai*: "Holy to God." How much more "seeing" would we do if we saw that way? For his part, Balaam opened his mouth after looking up and seeing Israel, and out came not a curse but a blessing, *Mah Tovu ohalecha Ya'akov, mishkenotecha Yisrael!* "How good are your tents, O Jacob, and your dwelling places O Israel!" Today, Jews around the world sing these words to open our morning prayer services when we are together in community. The foiled curse has become our blessing.

We do not all perceive our world in the same way, and our perceptions are often shaped by our expectations. Some of us see blessing where others see curse; some see hope and possibility where others see danger and overwhelming odds. When twelve men scouted the Promised Land and spied tall people living there, ten saw certain death. Convinced that Israel would fail against them, they described the people as giants and the land as one that consumes its inhabitants. But one of the scouts, Caleb, "because he was imbued with *a different spirit* and remained loyal to Me," saw an achievable goal and encouraged the people to enter the Promised Land (Num. 14:24).

All people experience fear of the unknown. But those who expect the worst will panic, and the few with a special kind of spirit, who expect that God will be with them always, remain calm even in the face of danger. Though we cannot control the nature of the spirit we've been given, we can control the ways in which we develop it. Just as David turned toward God again and again until God's spirit rested on him continually, we too can practice faith and hope in the midst of our fear. When ten spies saw catastrophe, Caleb saw a future. When the world is full of anxiety and sorrow, and cynical voices outnumber hopeful ones, we need those with spirits like Caleb's to speak up.

SPIRIT OF DEEP SLEEP: FORFEITING REVELATION

Every one of us has access to God's spirit for insight and understanding. Through God's spirit, we can pay attention to the smallest miracles all around us. Through God's spirit, we can sense what's right and understand how we are to live. Through God's spirit, we can see each other as holy beings created in God's image, and we can treat each other that way. Through God's spirit, we can trust even in the midst of our fear.

However, Tanakh also teaches that it is possible to stop paying attention, to go through the motions and forget why it is that we're here. The prophet Isaiah describes the effect of "a spirit of deep sleep" that can overtake us, stupefying us. We are alive, but we are not awake. This spirit closes us to deeper understanding, baffling us about how we ought to live, "so that all prophecy has been to you like the words of a sealed document" (Isa. 29:10).

We bring this spirit on ourselves, Isaiah proclaims, by serving God with our lips only and not with our hearts. "Because that people has approached Me with its mouth and honored Me with its lips, but has kept its heart far from Me, and its worship of Me has been a commandment of men learned by rote—truly I shall further baffle that people with bafflement upon bafflement; and the wisdom of its wise shall fail, and the prudence of its prudent shall vanish!" (Isa. 29:13–14). Isaiah is speaking to Israel, but like so much of the Hebrew Bible, this is a universal message. We human beings are capable of habituating ourselves to anything, even the service of God. We can go to our services and say all the right words while thinking about our business returns or what we'll make for dinner or whether our favorite show is on TV tonight. We can praise God for the majesty of creation and then despoil it; pray for justice and peace and then do nothing to alleviate poverty or bring an end to war. We can spend so much energy in earning and spending that we lose track of the deeper purpose for our existence.

What God is demanding through Isaiah is partnership. Receiving God's spirit is not a passive affair. If we want to understand revelation, we need to turn toward God and open our hearts toward understanding. The more we develop our capacity to listen, the more we hear. In his *Guide for the Perplexed*, Maimonides maintains that providence rests on all human beings, but not equally. The degree of providence given to each individual is graded to the degree that they have developed themselves. When we are born, we are not yet fully realized human beings, Maimonides says, but as we develop our intellects we actualize ourselves, fulfilling our purpose. God interacts with us to the degree that we develop our intellects. We reach toward God by developing ourselves intellectually, and God reaches toward us to the degree that we reach toward God.[45]

Spirit is a gift from God bestowed in extra measure on extraordinary leaders, artists, prophets, and heroes. *Ruach* gives its bearers courage and eloquence through highly developed qualities of wisdom, understanding, and knowledge of God. We have also seen that *ruach* is available in smaller measure to each of us, giving us insight and understanding. And we have seen that, with effort and attention, we can develop and grow the gift of *ruach* we receive. What are the implications for how we live our lives?

7
Finding Purpose Through Spirit

HEN WE FEEL FOR GOD'S SPIRIT AND listen for God's revelation vibrating from Sinai, we develop insights about how to live our lives—how to sensitize ourselves to ordinary miracles, how to awaken ourselves to the challenges and joys of being alive, how to treat other people with the respect that they deserve, how to see beyond our expectations. We also find that we have a purpose to fulfill in the world, a purpose based in a unique set of gifts belonging to every one of us. As we will see, these talents come through God's spirit, just as did the talents of the extraordinary leaders mentioned in Tanakh. We may not be Bezalel, chosen by name to build the Tabernacle, but each of us is gifted in our own way through spirit, and it is not only our option but also our obligation to bring those gifts to light.

THE COURAGE TO PURSUE PURPOSE

One of the most influential rabbis in the first and second centuries was Eliezer ben Hyrcanus. A compilation of rabbinic writings called *Avot d'Rabbi Natan*, from about the eighth century, includes fragments of Eliezer's life story. From it we can glean the following: Eliezer was born to a wealthy landowner named Hyrcanus. He had every advantage—land, silver, gold, the prospects of a good marriage. His life was comfortable and easy. But he was not satisfied. Somewhere deep down, Eliezer sensed that he had a purpose in the world that was going unfulfilled. He sensed that he had something to give. He couldn't articulate this for many years—he couldn't explain what was pulling on him—but he had a seemingly irrational desire to give his life to the study of Torah.

Everything in Eliezer's world seemed to pull back against what tugged on him. He was already twenty-eight years old and didn't even know the most basic prayers. His father and brothers did not care for Torah: they thought it impractical. There were no teachers of Torah near his home. Everyone expected that Eliezer would follow in the footsteps of his father as a powerful landowner.

How could he explain to his family what he knew he must do, and why he needed to walk away from the life they expected? It seemed impossible. We could imagine that Eliezer asked himself: "Who am I to have such grandiose ideas? What would my family do without me?" Day after day he struggled inside as he did his best to live up to his father's expectations.

Avot d'Rabbi Natan records that one day, when he was out with his father plowing the land, Eliezer began to weep. He crumpled to the ground, racked with sobs. It was clear that he could not pretend anymore that plowing the land was his purpose. When his father came to see what was wrong, Eliezer gathered his courage and told the truth: "I wish to study Torah." Eliezer's father thought this was ludicrous, but he did not stop his son.

Eliezer made his way, alone, to Jerusalem. He arrived at the study hall of Yohanan ben Zakkai and dedicated the rest of his life to the study of Torah.[46]

Perhaps this has happened to you. You have known that there is something you are meant to do, some purpose that you must fulfill. Perhaps you are living your purpose, and a sense of calling led you to the work you do today. You had the courage to pluck yourself out of another life, a more comfortable life, to follow your sense of purpose. Or perhaps your courageous move still lies ahead.

There are people all around us who have a yearning inside, who have a dream they've written off as crazy or postponed for some future day when they can find the courage to leap. For some, there's a sense of something missing, an abiding question: what am I here for?

There are moments in life when it is clear what we must do, how we must live. Perhaps you were walking the dog, or picking out cereal for your kids at the grocery store, or sitting on the freeway during the morning commute. Something came over the radio, or you were remembering a conversation from last night, or it appeared entirely out of the blue. Your heart quickened as it felt truth. Your mind started to race. "Yes, yes of course. I knew this, I merely forgot." Then there was a feeling of resolve. "I will change to live this truth. I will do what I am meant to do. I will live up to my calling, my purpose. To make of my life a blessing. I can, and I will."

Then the obstacles parade themselves before us. "How would we pay the bills? What would my workmates do without me? What if I can't pull it off? What will the kids do in the afternoons?

Who do I think I am anyway?" We step away from the dream. Imperceptibly at first. It is still there, but it has lost its power. Maybe it was a crazy idea after all.

Perhaps the dream lingers as a hopeful reverie, something to distract us from the humdrum of the day. Perhaps it is entirely forgotten, lost until the next time it pops out from behind the cereal boxes.

Many of us are hiding. We are hiding our gifts. We are hiding from God's spirit. We are hiding from the responsibility to live our purpose. When Adam and Eve hide in the garden of Eden after eating the fruit, God asks a question that echoes throughout human history. *Ayeka?* "Where are you?"

The Source of Life is calling us. We are being summoned with dreams and expectations that we think we cannot fulfill. Every one of us has a purpose, something we are meant to do in the world. We know that there is something we have to offer, something we must give of ourselves. And we all doubt whether we can do it. We are all afraid. But when we find our purpose and have the courage to give it to the greater good, we find that we are gifted, and we begin to shine.

One day, months or perhaps years into Eliezer's studies, there was a great celebration in the study hall of Yohanan ben Zakkai. When Yohanan asked Eliezer to teach words of Torah to this illustrious group, Eliezer demurred. How could he, a new student, possibly teach Torah to these great men? He wanted to hide. "To what can my situation be compared?" he taught. He turned to his teacher and said: "To a cistern that cannot put forth more water than it has received. Similarly, I cannot say more words of Torah than I have received from you." Yohanan replied with his own parable. "To what can your situation be compared? To a fountain which flows and from which water comes and which can give out more water than it receives. Similarly you can utter more words of Torah than were received on Mount Sinai." Yohanan saw how gifted Eliezer was, even if Eliezer could not see it himself. Eliezer then expounded words of Torah, and he did so brilliantly. The story records: "His face was shining like sunlight, [there were] rays shooting out like the rays of Moses so that no man could know whether it was day or night."[47]

When Eliezer stood plowing the land with his father, he knew he belonged somewhere else. In a place beyond words, beyond rational language, Eliezer knew that there was something he was meant to do with his life. He couldn't know then, standing on that rocky hillside, that he was gifted as a teacher of Torah. He just knew, he felt through the spirit within him, that he had a purpose that he had to fulfill. And he was right. God's spirit was speaking through Eliezer, pulling him to do what he was meant to do in the world.

DISCERNING THE GIFTS

Not everyone is Eliezer. There are many people who do not yet have a sense of purpose, who do not feel themselves called to do something specific with their lives. For some it begins with a gift. In Exodus 28:3, God tells Moses: "Next you shall instruct all who are skillful, all whom I have given a skill [literally, "whom I have filled with the spirit of wisdom"]." We each have gifts within us, gifts that we discover over the course of our lives. Given that every one of us has some measure of *ruach* within us, every one of us is gifted.

We have all known people who seem to possess an extra measure of insight, an ability to see underlying meaning within a course of events. In the book of Genesis, Joseph is one of these people. As a youth Joseph knows that he has a gift, and he is proud of himself. As he relates his dreams to his brothers and his father, we can see the young Joseph strutting around in his multicolored tunic, chest puffed, a smug look on his face. Though he knows he has a gift, he doesn't know what it's for. Unlike Eliezer, Joseph does not yet have a sense of purpose. He thinks his gift is all about him, and he uses his gift only for himself, without regard for his brothers.

There are consequences to this behavior, and Joseph suffers them—his brothers throw him into a pit, and then they sell him to travelers, who take him down to Egypt. But he learns from his time in the pit, and we can learn with him. The Rabbis taught, "Humankind was created from a single ancestor to show the grandeur of the Holy Blessed One, for . . . the Blessed Holy One, minted all human beings with the same stamp . . . yet not one of us is like anyone else. Therefore, we are each obligated to maintain, 'On my account the world was created!'" (Mishnah *Sanhedrin* 4:5).

Joseph learns that he is merely a vessel to fulfill God's purpose. He realizes that his entirely unique gifts come from God. If each of us is obligated to maintain, "On my account the world was created!" then each of us is necessary for creation itself, and each of us is obligated to ask ourselves: what do I have inside me that must be given to the world? Joseph realizes that his very existence demands that he give what he has to give and use it for creation itself.

When he reappears in Egypt, Joseph's understanding of himself has changed. As we read of Potiphar, Joseph's master there: "His master saw that Adonai was with him, and Adonai made everything that he did succeed in his hand" (Gen. 39:3). How did Potiphar, an Egyptian, come to attribute Joseph's success to Adonai, a God he did not know? The medieval commentator Rashi says that what Potiphar saw was that "the name of heaven was always on his [Joseph's] lips." Potiphar saw and heard Joseph speak the name of his God and attribute his success and abilities not to his own powers but to his God.[48]

When Joseph uses his gifts for others, interpreting the dreams of the baker and cupbearer while he is in prison, and later the dreams of Pharaoh himself, he finds that he saves all of Egypt, and his own family as well. When he interprets Pharaoh's dream, we read, "And Pharaoh said to his courtiers, 'Could we find another like him, a man in whom is the spirit of God?'" (Gen. 41:38).

Pharaoh's question is a good one: do we all have access to gifts like Joseph's? The Talmud states that *ruach hakodesh* ("the holy spirit") ceased to exist after the death of the last prophets, but teachers like Rabbi Aryeh Kaplan insist that this only applies to the higher levels of prophecy. A lower-level gift of prophecy, such as interpreting dreams, Kaplan states, "is attainable by any person, at any time or place, as long as the person makes himself worthy of it."[49] Thus Joseph teaches us that when we let our gifts shine, when we give our gifts to a greater good, we find our holy purpose. Every time we move toward our sense of purpose, every time we bring a gift out of hiding, every time we take a risk, we gain courage for the next leap. And we embolden others to do the same.

REVEALING OURSELVES

God's spirit gives us gifts and a sense of purpose, and Tanakh teaches that it is also God's spirit that enables us to discern what we've been given and what we have to give the world. "The spirit [*neshamah*] of man is the light of Adonai revealing all his inmost parts" (Prov. 20:27). This proverb could be interpreted in a couple of ways: that our *neshamah* is a light within us that enables us to know ourselves and what we have to give; and that our *neshamah* enables us to know God's, that our *neshamah* is our intimate link with the Infinite One. These are related. The more we understand the gifts within us given by God, the nature of our souls, the more we know God. Given that our *neshamah* and *ruach* are given by God, intimate knowledge of them is our most accessible means for intimate knowledge of God.

Those without a religious life often say that one does not need to believe in God or to go to synagogue or church to know right from wrong, that one does not need to study Torah or Bible to understand how to live in the world. We all have within us a moral compass that enables us to sense how to behave. Our society has laws that prohibit antisocial behavior. Our parents and teachers show us how to get along with others and teach us the values we need to find our way through the world. Why do we need religion?

Of course, the laws of our country are derived from Torah and the Christian Bible as they influenced the governments of Europe and the West. The values that Americans take for granted are, by and large, Jewish and Christian values deriving originally from Tanakh and the New Testament. But Judaism actually teaches that it is not at all simple to live a good life. It takes great attention and hard work. We all have within us two inclinations. These inclinations that pull us toward action for good and action for bad are labeled *yetzer tov* and *yetzer ra*. According to Jewish tradition, we are not born with original sin or with a natural propensity to do wrong. We are born with a pure *neshamah*, a clean slate, and instincts in both directions.

We study Torah to go beyond the surface of the laws and customs of our society, to consider more deeply the ways in which we are obligated and how we ought to live. When Jews study Torah, we use God's spirit within us to endeavor to move beyond the surface or obvious meaning, called *p'shat*. Like the surface of our table, the surface of the text shows us one dimension of the full story. We expect that there are layers hidden beneath the surface of each phrase, each word, and each letter. Jewish tradition teaches that there are four layers to Torah and, really, all of existence. *P'shat* is the literal, contextual, and obvious meaning of the text. Beneath *p'shat* is *remez*, meaning "hint." *Remez* is something implied, something pointing at deeper truth in the text. Beneath *remez* is *drash*, a searching out. *Drash* (root of the word *midrash*) is an allegorical or homiletical meaning of the text. *Drash* often makes a connection between one text and another in Tanakh—it is a search for associative meaning. Finally, beneath *drash* is *sod* (with a long *o*), the secret, hidden, or mystical meaning of the text. At the *sod* level, the text is read like a code containing another text within.

Though study is the foundation of all that we do, it is not near-ly enough. It is through the acts of *mitzvot* that we experience the values that underlie them. When we visit the sick, or accompany those who are mourning, or pay a day laborer his due on the day that he works, or take a break from the frenzy of our commercial culture one day a week, we come to understand the values of compassion, community, economic justice, and rest. When the Israelites beheld God's presence at Sinai, their first response was *na'aseh v'nishmah*: we will do and we will hear. Why "do" first and "hear" later? Because it is through doing that the words make sense. And that way, our words should never outstrip our deeds.

In much of life, it is not simple or easy to do the right thing. Take, for example, a basic and necessary act: eating. We eat not only for survival but also because food tastes good. Judaism is not an ascetic tradition—we value the physical pleasures of life, including (some would say especially) eating. But how should we eat? There are myriad Jewish texts exploring this question, and it is not possible in this short space to do them justice. If we eat animals, are there some that are inappropriate? How should they be raised and killed? How do we express gratitude to God for our food and for the experience of being sated? Are we obligated not to overeat? What is our responsibility to share our food? Even if we know the "correct" answers to these and many other questions related to food, it isn't easy to simply do the right thing. What if we have a craving for food that's out of bounds? What if we're hungry and it's the only food around? What if we're guests at someone else's home? Many situations require nuance in our commitments, and we often must weigh competing values. If we look deeply at our actions, we see that "doing the right thing" is both complicated and difficult. Striving to do good, to keep our deeds ahead of our words, is a continual process of action and reflection.

We each hear God in our own way. What Israel heard echoing from Sinai is a call to action—commanded, righteous action. As heirs to that experience, we continue to listen inside for our sense of purpose. We have the humility to serve what is larger than us through study of Torah, and we strive to fulfill our obligations to others through *mitzvot*. There is a Hasidic story that a person should walk around with two slips of paper, one in each pocket. On one slip it is written, "I am nothing more than dust and ashes." On the other, "The whole world was created for me." Our task is to find the balance between the humility that knows we are a blink of existence serving a mission much greater than our own and the awe that we were created as beings of infinite value, here for a purpose.

Our task is to use the measure of *ruach* we've been given to reach for understanding, to look for miracle, to listen for God, to discern beneath the surface of life our portion of God's purpose. Some people have been given an extra measure of *ruach*, enabling them to do extraordinary things. All of us have been given enough to be able to understand God's revelation—to align ourselves with God's greater purpose, making ourselves instruments to do good.

PART THREE

Redemption: Aspiring to Wholeness

8
Deliverance and Demand:
God's Redemptive Spirit

WE HAVE SEEN IN TORAH THAT GOD'S spirit helped to birth the world, bring humanity to life, and give humans understanding of God and the purpose of our existence. In the dimension of *creation*, we feel God's spirit within us as we breathe, keeping us alive and giving us a connection to the source of our lives. In the dimension of *revelation*, we feel God's spirit as inspiration as we move from existence to awareness to insight to a sense of purpose. God's spirit opens a line of communication between humanity and the divine, enabling human beings to understand how we are to live and to contribute ourselves to our world.

The dimension of *redemption* is fueled by our aspirations for wholeness. We exist, we understand, and therefore we strive. Alive and awake, we find ourselves in a partnership with God with a shared imperative—to heal and repair our world. It is not enough to breathe. It is not enough to feel inspired by miracles and seek wisdom. We cannot be satisfied. Presenting us with a vision of how the world should be, God demands that we aspire to bring that world into being.

The story of the Jewish people's slavery in Egypt teaches that in the night of utter despair God's spirit is not only with us, but God's spirit is also what will release us. Once we are free, able to breathe deeply and full of spirit once again, we will never again forget what it was like to be strangers, despised, short of *ruach*. If we become comfortable again, if we are ever complacent, we will find that God's spirit tugs at us, calls us, to risk what we have for truth. God demands that we be holy, for God is holy. And as we'll see, God's holiness is defined as a passionate concern for those at the margins—the stranger and the powerless. "The stranger who resides with you shall be to you as one of your citizens; you shall love him as yourself," God demands, "for you were strangers in the land of Egypt" (Lev. 19:34). This is the lesson: there's a demand in the bargain of delivery. Once we have been saved from the crush of oppression, redeemed, we belong to God. And we will forever be expected to save others as we were saved. Just when we want to mind our own business, just when we want to do what is easy, we will forever be expected to "go forth," to be holy.

GOING OUT OF EGYPT *(YETZIAT MITZRAYIM)*

Every Spring, at the holiday of Passover, Jews gather with family and friends to recount the story of the Exodus from Egypt. Passover, or *Pesach* in Hebrew, is by far the most observed holiday on the Jewish calendar. Jews who do not go to synagogue, Jews who do not believe in God, Jews who do nothing else Jewish throughout the year nevertheless gather to sit around the Passover seder table with parents, grandparents, children, sisters, brothers, cousins, neighbors, and friends to tell the story of our people's liberation from slavery. The Passover story is *the* Jewish story, the defining Jewish narrative. In Hebrew it is called *Yetziat Mitzrayim*. *Yetziat* means "going out," and the Hebrew word for Egypt, *Mitzrayim*, means "the narrow place." Thus, the Exodus becomes a metaphor for all forms of escape from oppression, release from all of the narrow places ruled by the despots of our world.

The Exodus has been our people's source of hope in every age, under every form of oppression and threat. In antiquity, under the Roman Empire, when our rabbis were martyred and blood ran in the streets, our people told the story of the Exodus. Under the Spanish Inquisition, when we were tortured, killed, and exiled, we told the story of the Exodus. In Italy, when locked behind the iron gates of the ghetto, we told the story of the Exodus. In Medieval Europe, under threat of the blood libel (when mobs massacred Jews on the claim that we used the blood of Christian babies to make matzah), we still told the story of the Exodus. In the shtetls of Russia, under threat of pogroms (massacres) and conscription into the czar's army, our people told the story of the Exodus. Even in the concentration camps of Nazi Germany, our people told the story of the Exodus.

Ninety-year-old Pearl Benisch, living now in Brooklyn, told Joan Nathan in the *New York Times* that she remembers Passover in the Bergen-Belsen concentration camp in the spring of 1945, just days before her liberation. "We had nothing to eat but watery soup, with bread once a week," she said in a quiet voice. "But I was one of the lucky ones. I was working in a place where we peeled potatoes and turnips. I cut three turnips in narrow rounds, covered them up with a piece of brown paper and hid them in my shoes. When we had our seder in the peeling room with one woman keeping watch for the guards, the other women moaned that there was no matzo. I said, 'they are here, they are under the cover.' They opened the brown paper and there were the three round turnip matzos." Then Mrs. Benisch paused and said in a whisper, "Only God can make matzo from turnips."[50]

The Exodus story has served as a powerful parable for oppressed peoples and liberation movements around the world, including of course the American civil rights movement. Who does not know the story of baby Moses in the basket on the River Nile? Raised in Pharaoh's palace, he learns that his Hebrew brethren are beyond the palace gates, enslaved. In his rage, he kills a taskmaster, flees to Midian, encounters God at the burning bush, and returns to face Pharaoh to help liberate his people through God's ten plagues and the crossing of the Sea of Reeds (Red Sea). At the Passover seder, we imagine what it would be like to know nothing but slavery, to live in a time or place where no one could remember freedom. We taste the tears of our ancestors with parsley dipped in salt water. We ingest the bitterness of slavery with the bitter herbs. We reenact the impoverishment of our ancestors and the haste of their escape with matzah. And we also take the story to its redemptive point as we, in contrast, recline at our meal, drink four cups of wine, and eat the sweet *charoset* (apples, nuts, and honey), remembering that we are now free.

God's *ruach* appears twice in the Exodus story, first to bring the eighth plague, after blood, frogs, lice, insects, cattle disease, boils, and hail had failed to convince Pharaoh to let the people go. Each time, Pharaoh asked that the plague be reversed, and once it was reversed he forbade the Hebrews to go. "Then Adonai said to Moses, 'Hold out your arm over the land of Egypt for the locusts, that they may come upon the land of Egypt and eat up all the grasses in the land, whatever the hail has left.' So Moses held out his rod over the land of Egypt, and the Eternal drove a *ruach kadim* ["east wind"] over the land all that day and all night; and when morning came, the *ruach kadim* had brought the locusts" (Exod. 10:12–13).

The splitting of the Sea of Reeds, perhaps the grandest miracle in all of Torah, was accomplished with another *ruach kadim*. "Then Moses held out his arm over the sea and Adonai drove back the sea with a strong *ruach kadim* all that night, and turned the sea into dry ground" (Exod. 14:21). Notice the parallel with Genesis 1:2, when *ruach Elohim* hovered over the surface of the water, dividing the water, and eventually creating dry land. Jewish commentators, for the most part, have defined the *ruach kadim* as a natural phenomenon, a strong eastern wind that blew over many hours to push back the waters. However, the word *kadim* also means "ancient" or "original." The nineteenth-century Hasidic master Levi Yitzhak of Berdichev translates *ruach kadim* as "ancient wind," saying, "God does not change or suspend the laws of nature in order to work miracles. The wind that divided the sea had been created for that purpose at the time of the creation of the world."[51]

What split the Sea of Reeds? Was it a natural wind blowing from the east? Did God cause a wind to blow, a wind separate from God but under God's control? Was it God's wind, like God's breath blowing away the waters? Or was it God's spirit moving from the east, the place of origins, just like it hovered on the primordial waters of creation to separate them?

In the Song of the Sea, immediately following their crossing, the Israelites rejoice, "At the blast of your nostrils the waters piled up, the floods stood straight like a wall; the deeps froze in the heart of the sea. The foe said, 'I will pursue, I will overtake, I will divide the spoil; My desire shall have its fill of them. I will bare my sword—My hand shall subdue them.' You made Your wind blow, the sea covered them; They sank like lead in the majestic waters" (Exod. 15:8–10). In their song the Israelites describe the wind that split the sea as God's own breath.

Today, Jews in the West often put a special work of art on the eastern wall of their homes, the wall facing Jerusalem, to remind them of their relationship to our ancient home. Such works of art are called *mizrach*, meaning "east." A play on the word *mizrach*, *mi-tzad zeh ruach ha-chayim*, is often included in the artwork. *Mi-tzad zeh ruach ha-chayim* means, "from this direction comes the spirit of life." From the east, the place of origins, comes *ruach kadim*, a spirit of life.

Whatever it was that split the Sea of Reeds—God's wind, God's breath, God's spirit—it enabled the Israelites to make the long walk from slavery to freedom, inspiring hope in oppressed people ever since.

LECH L'CHA: ABRAHAM'S JOURNEY

When we speak about redemption, we speak about what God does and what we do. God's spirit is right at the center of both— enabling us to see what's not right in the world and moving us to do something about it.

Have you ever suddenly seen, in sharp and bright and undeniable clarity, that some part of the way you have been living, the way everyone around you has been living, is wrong? That something you were taught was right and natural and good, something you took for granted and never questioned, was based on a lie? In that moment, you knew that you could not go on living as you had. Maybe you also knew that you had to speak out, to act, to do something to change the course of events. This was the experience of the Hebrew prophets, who were plucked out of their lives to carry a message that struck to the core of the societies in which they lived. This was the experience of many early abolitionists opposing American slavery, and the opponents of segregation one hundred years later.

If you have had a moment like this—about anything—perhaps it came through reading a book, or hearing a lecture, or seeing the conditions yourself. Perhaps everything got very quiet, and you heard a whisper that was truer than anything you had heard before, and you knew you had to follow it.

The Midrash teaches that when he hears God's words to "go forth," Avram (as he was then known) had known for some time that idols are not gods but merely small statues of clay. He knew that there is only one God in the universe. And he knew that the way he had been living, working in an idol shop and selling these false gods to the people around him, was wrong. Then, suddenly, Avram heard the whisper of God.

What he heard was a somewhat mysterious construction—*Lech L'cha*. What does it mean? When translated as "Go forth, get on with you, go away"—we imagine this opening command as merely the launching of a journey. But some commentators hear loneliness in these words. The modern commentator Nehama Leibowitz translates *Lech L'cha* as, "Get thee out," placing a barrier, she says, between Avram and the rest of the world.[52] Samson Raphael Hirsch suggests that the Hebrew implies, "Go by yourself," describing what Hirsch calls "the aloneness of Abraham."[53] And, as we know, the rest of the command wrenches Avram from his land, his people, and his family.

Standing up for what we know to be true when most people around us don't want to hear it carries risk—of losing friendships, reputation, belonging, even family. And that is why we are reluctant to open ourselves to our role in redemption, to see the wrong that is before us, to hear the cry of the orphan and the widow and the stranger. Even when we've done it before, perhaps especially when we've done it before, it takes a special courage to face the risk, the potential loss.

A Hasidic rabbi, Mordechai Yosef of Isbitza, interpreted *Lech L'cha* to mean, "Go forth to learn who you are meant to be." The Jewish tradition teaches us to have the lonely courage not to close our ears to truth or look away but to listen for the whisper, keep our eyes on the glimmer, to that clear and sharp and undeniable knowing of what we must do.

BE HOLY, FOR I AM HOLY

If we are willing to take the risk to follow truth, if we are willing to launch a journey in pursuit of justice, how can we be sure that it is God's spirit guiding us and not our own fancy? How can we know what God's spirit would want us to do?

If you roll a Torah scroll to its very center, you will find there, in the midst of the book of Leviticus, the Holiness Code. *Kedoshim Tihiyu*, the Holiness Code begins. "Be holy, for I Adonai your God, am holy." Jews are commanded to strive for holiness in imitation of God. But what does it mean, then, that God is holy? And what does it look like for human beings to be holy?

When, in the next book of Torah, Korach gathers a band of 250 men to rebel against Moses, he makes the claim, based on a misunderstanding of the Holiness Code, that all of the people are holy and that therefore they should have power. The idea of a chosen people is often misunderstood, and was by the likes of Korach, to mean special or deserving of privilege. Each people is chosen in its own way. For the Israelites, and the Jewish people, being chosen and striving for holiness means being obligated to the people on the margins of society.

Immediately following the command to be holy, the Torah lists a series of *mitzvot*. This list includes some of the highlights of the Ten Commandments—honor mother and father, keep Shabbat, do not steal. But the list is a little different from the one the Israelites received on carved tablets amid smoke and cloud. This one gives special attention to our obligations to others—the poor, the hungry, the stranger, the day laborer, the deaf, the blind, the old. "When you reap the harvest of your land, you shall not reap all the way to the edges of the field, or gather the gleanings of your harvest. You shall not pick your vineyard bare, or gather the fallen fruit of your vineyard; you shall leave them for the poor and the stranger: I the Lord am your God" (Lev. 19:9–10). If we imagine an agricultural society in which most people are subsistence farmers, the Torah is demanding that these farmers leave food that they could use to feed their families for the nourishment of the stranger and the poor. This is a structural commitment in the society to ensure that no person goes hungry.

Holiness is how we relate to the most vulnerable in the society, the most marginalized—the people we could most easily get away with harming, ignoring, or cheating. "You shall not insult the deaf, or place a stumbling block before the blind. You shall fear your God: I am Adonai" (Lev. 19:14). We are told in the Holiness Code that we may not defraud our fellow; we may not keep the wages of a laborer until morning. We must ensure justice for all. We may not hate our fellow human being. *V'ahavta l'reacha kamocha*: "Love your fellow human being as yourself." This is what a holy person does. This is what it means to live in imitation of God's holiness.

When we say that God is holy, we mean that God is listening to the cry of the most oppressed in any society, that God's spirit will act, independently and through humanity, "to unlock the fetters of wickedness, and untie the cords of the yoke, to let the oppressed go free" (Isa. 58:6).

Holiness is not abstract. It is not subtle. It is visible, concrete action—action not for ourselves but for other people. This is what it means for God to be holy, Torah teaches, and this is what it means for us to be holy: to take ethical action, action that creates a system of justice and greater equality in society. But it is not easy for people to consistently care for the stranger, for the poor, for the weak, for the marginalized, and that is why we need prophets guided by God's spirit to remind us of our obligation to reach for holiness.

9
The Role of Spirit in Prophecy

AS WE STRIVE TO CONTRIBUTE TO THE GREAT drama of redemption, to be holy, fulfilling our part of covenant, we need help. We need someone to shake us awake, to remind us of what must be done, and to hold out a vision of the world as it could be. This is what the prophets give us, and we will find that they rely on God's spirit for both voice and vision.

As Abraham Joshua Heschel says in his authoritative book on the prophets, "Our eyes are witness to the callousness and cruelty of man, but our heart tries to obliterate the memories, to calm the nerves, and to silence our conscience."[54] We all see suffering around us. We are overwhelmed by images of suffering, by examples of suffering in our cities and in the farthest reaches of our world. What do we do about it? Do we change the pattern of our lives to uproot and end this suffering, or do we continue with business as usual while others are sleeping on the streets, locked in prisons, hungry at night, living in despair?

We can understand how people go on living with dissonance between their values and the reality of their surroundings. We do not want people to be homeless. We do not want people to be hungry. We do not want people to grow up without hope. But sometimes we ask ourselves, what can I do to change it? We need to take care of our own families, which means that we need to work and that we are busy. If we lived in Israel at the time of the Hebrew prophets, they would be yelling at us. The Hebrew prophets were dramatic and relentless, desperately trying to get the people to listen.

This is because the prophets could hear as God hears the suffering among the marginalized, and they were compelled to speak. Heschel continues, "Prophecy is the voice that God has lent to the silent agony, a voice to the plundered poor, to the profaned riches of the world." As we become inured to the suffering around us by force of habit and the need for our survival, as we rationalize the conditions of the poor and the persistence of our inaction, "the prophet is intent on intensifying responsibility, is impatient of excuse, contemptuous of pretense and self-pity." When we stop listening, tune out, become accustomed to seeing the men with little cardboard signs at the freeway exit or under the highway overpass, "the prophet's ear . . . is attuned to a cry imperceptible to others," and it amplifies that cry so that we will listen.

For some prophets, it is God's *ruach* that inspires them to speak. For others, God's *ruach* literally lifts them out of ordinary life and carries them away to have visions and to speak on behalf of God. Some prophets see God's *ruach* bringing redemption to the world, or punishing the people for abrogating their part of covenant, for choosing greed and individual ambition over collective redemption. When the Israelites fail to live up to a high standard of behavior, to partner with God in redemptive action, it is God's *ruach* that inspires our collective conscience through the prophetic voice, and it is God's *ruach* that empowers us to recommit to bringing a redeemed world.

MICAH: THE COURAGE TO SPEAK

Avram had the lonely courage to pick up his life and give up everything he knew to start a new nation. The prophet Micah had a different kind of courage—to speak truth to power. To expose corruption, denounce fraud, and confront the land barons of his day with the voices of the hungry and the landless and the poor.

Micah lived in the eighth century BCE, during the reigns of King Jotham, Ahaz, and Hezekiah. He lived in the town of Moreshet, in a rural area southwest of Jerusalem. Unlike his contemporary, Isaiah, who walked the corridors of the palace and spoke directly to the king, Micah lived in the country with the poor and downtrodden. Micah saw large landowners forcibly take the land of their neighbors and use their power to secure rulings in their interests. The wealthy landowners around him were powerful and intimidating, and it was not easy for Micah to find the courage to speak out against their unethical actions.

It was through God's spirit that Micah saw clearly what needed to change in Israel, and it was through God's spirit that he had the fortitude to confront his society. "But I, I am filled with strength by the spirit of Adonai and with judgment and courage, to declare to Jacob his transgressions and to Israel his sin" (Mic. 3:8). Micah railed against the corruption he saw at every level of the society—among not only landowners but also judges, priests, and prophets. "Hear this, you rulers of the House of Jacob, You chiefs of the House of Israel, who detest justice and make crooked all that is straight, who build Zion with crime, Jerusalem with iniquity! Her rulers judge for gifts, Her priests give rulings for a fee, And her prophets divine for pay" (Mic. 3:9–11).

Micah attributed to God's spirit not only his courage to inveigh against the wrongs of his time but also his ability to give the people a vision of righteous action: "What Adonai requires of you: Only to do justice, and to love goodness, and to walk modestly with your God" (Mic. 6:8).

We are not prophets, but we can be the kind of people that the prophets urge us to be. We cannot hear the sound of suffering with the degree of sensitivity that God gave the prophets, but we can still listen. We cannot produce signs and wonders to convince our neighbors and fellow citizens to change their ways, but we can use the gift of speech to call attention to the wrongs that we see in the world.

EZEKIEL: CARRIED AWAY BY SPIRIT

While God's spirit gives Micah the strength to speak against injustice, it is still Micah himself making the choice to speak. With the prophet Ezekiel, however, we see an experience of God's spirit that is completely overpowering. Ezekiel tells us that he is literally carried away by God's spirit. According to Ezekiel, God's spirit overtakes him, filling him with visions, physically moving him from place to place and causing him to prophesy, even against his own will.

Ezekiel prophesied in the early sixth century BCE, at the time of the destruction of the first Temple in Jerusalem. Ezekiel was one of three thousand Jews who were exiled from Jerusalem with King Jehoiachin by the Babylonians. The prophet lived most of his life in exile, and he addressed his prophecies to the exile community living in Babylonia.

Ezekiel credited his ability to hear God's voice to spirit: "As He spoke to me, a spirit entered into me and set me upon my feet; and I heard what was being spoken to me" (Ezek. 2:1–2). He describes spirit lifting him into God's presence: "Then a spirit carried me away, and behind me I heard a great roaring sound, 'Blessed is the Presence of Adonai in His place'" (Ezek. 3:12). Just two verses later, Ezekiel describes spirit taking him against his own will: "A spirit seized me and carried me away. I went in bitterness, in the fury of my spirit, while the hand of Adonai was strong upon me" (Ezek. 3:14). And it is through God's spirit that Ezekiel becomes God's messenger: "The spirit of Adonai fell upon me, and He said to me, 'Speak: Thus said Adonai . . .'" (Ezek. 11:5). Finally, it is God's spirit that creates Ezekiel's visions and brings him to the exile community to transmit them. "A spirit carried me away and brought me in a vision by the spirit of God to the exile community in Chaldea" (Ezek. 11:24).

We get the sense from his own testimony that Ezekiel is no more than a conduit for the spirit of God. Unlike Micah, Ezekiel does not have agency. He is unable to resist or to change what is said. The spirit of God seizes him, moves him, fills him with words, and causes him to speak. In Ezekiel's experience, God's spirit controls every aspect of prophecy.

Through God's spirit, Ezekiel has powerful visions of redemption that he shares with the exile community. As we'll see, God's spirit is central to each of these visions for a redeemed people and a redeemed world.

A HEART OF FLESH

Like all of the prophets before him, Ezekiel expresses disappointment with the people Israel. They have failed to live up to covenant. They have disappointed God, because their hearts are like stone. They fail to feel the suffering of those around them. They fail to care about their relationship with God. But, God insists through Ezekiel, the people are not doomed. God will replace the people's stony hearts with sensitive organs that feel and respond to the world around them. "I will give them one heart and put a new spirit in them; I will remove the heart of stone from their bodies and give them a heart of flesh" (Ezek. 11:19). "And I will give you a new heart and put a new spirit into you: I will remove the heart of stone from your body and give you a heart of flesh; and I will put my spirit into you. Thus I will cause you to follow My laws and faithfully to observe My rules" (Ezek. 36:26–27).

In each of these iterations, we see a symbiotic relationship intimated between heart and spirit—as a heart of flesh is given, it is accompanied by a new spirit. In Biblical times, the heart was thought to be not only the center of emotion but also the seat of the intellect. Thus, a stone heart is not only cold and unfeeling, not only selfish, but also unyielding, unresponsive, and unwise. A stone heart is hard and closed, lacking the ability to learn from criticism, to change and improve. Rashi describes a heart of flesh as "soft and ready to submit"—no longer strong-willed and stubborn but yielding to a will and wisdom greater than its own.

We learned earlier that our spirits bring us insight, awareness, sensitivity, wisdom, understanding, and knowledge. When we studied Bezalel and revelation, we saw understanding defined as the ability to integrate in our hearts the wisdom drawn in through our spirits. It seems, then, that heart and spirit are deeply inter-related—spirit is the access point for these qualities, and heart is where they grow and develop. If our hearts are stone—hard and closed—our spirits cannot function. They can no longer receive revelation. But when we receive new hearts and new spirits, body and spirit can work together once again to grow in understanding and turn toward righteous action.

POURING OUT OF SPIRIT

When calamity has befallen the Jewish people, it has felt as if we were abandoned by God. In Tanakh, God is described as hiding God's face in a terrifying portrait of estrangement—the prophets imagine God turning away from us, as we have turned away from God. Ezekiel's prophetic vision counters this bleak image, acknowledging our experience of abandonment while also promising a future safe from it: "I will never again hide My face from them, for I will pour out My spirit on the House of Israel—declares Adonai God" (Ezek. 39:29).

What is the relationship between God's turned face and God's spirit? We might describe God's turning away as a withholding of *ruach*, making us short of breath and shallow in understanding. When they were enslaved in Egypt, the Hebrews suffered from *kotser ruach*, shortness of breath or shrunken spirit. In contrast, when God pours out God's *ruach*, spirit does not just rest on us, it is not merely placed on us: we are showered, enveloped, embraced with God's spirit. We breathe deeply. A nineteenth-century commentator known as Malbim imagines the pouring out of spirit as the gift of prophecy for all the people: "The holy spirit will return to the people with the power of prophecy."[55]

REVIVAL OF THE DRY BONES

Even when all seems lost, when it seems that redemption is impossible, God's spirit is with us and redemption will still come. This is the meaning of Ezekiel's prophecy of the dry bones. No matter how bad it gets, in what depths of oppression we find ourselves, whether it is four hundred years of slavery in Egypt or hundreds of years of Crusades and pogroms—even after the Holocaust—the message of our tradition is that redemption will come. Even if, God forbid, one day we are nothing more than a valley of bones, as the people Israel must have felt while in exile after the destruction of the Temple, Ezekiel is telling us that redemption will still come.

We will see that throughout this story and even in the specific moment when the dry bones are revived, *ruach* is used in all three of its meanings—wind, breath, and spirit. It takes a combination of all three to return the dead to life. "The hand of the Eternal came upon me. He took me out by the spirit of Adonai and set me down in the valley. It was full of bones" (Ezek. 37:1). Perhaps if we take the dry bones as metaphor for all of the desiccated dreams we see around us in our society, all of the wasted lives waiting for revival, we can relate to how overwhelming it would be to stand in a valley of dry bones with the hope of resurrecting them. "He said to me, 'O mortal, can these bones live again?'" (37:3): Do you believe, looking out at all of this devastation in our world, that we can ever repair it all, that we can ever restore hope and life to the dead and dying places in our world?

"And He said to me, 'Prophesy over these bones and say to them: O dry bones, hear the word of Adonai!'" (37:4). Why did God need Ezekiel to play a role in the revival of the bones? They were not alive, so why did they need a messenger? They would eventually be revived through God's wind, breath, and spirit, in addition to Ezekiel's speech. What was the role of the mortal in this miracle? Representing the spiritual death of Israel in exile, this story asserts that even the most down and out can be revived; even out of the pits of despair, the farthest reaches of exile, an entire people can rise again, return home, and parent new generations. But God cannot, or will not, do this alone. God needs partners, mortal partners, to contribute to the revitalization of the mortal world.

"Thus said Adonai God to these bones: I will cause *ruach* to enter you and you shall live again. . . . And I will put *ruach* into you, and you shall live again. And you shall know that I am Adonai!" (37:5–6). Is God promising breath or spirit, or both, to revive the bones? Perhaps, as in the creation of humanity in Genesis 2:7, it is life breath, breath and spirit combined, that God will breathe into these bones. Just as we were first made living beings with God's life breath in our nostrils, so we are reborn.

Ezekiel prophesied as God commanded him, and the bones came together, with sinews, flesh, and skin, "but there was no *ruach* in them" (37:8). Malbim comments, "Everything was formed, but the spirit of life cannot enter bodies through prophets, only through God Himself."[56]

Then God commands Ezekiel to speak to the *ruach*: "'Thus said the Eternal God: Come, O *ruach*, from the four winds, and breathe into these slain that they may live again.' I prophesied as He commanded me. The *ruach* entered them, and they came to life and stood up on their feet, a vast multitude" (37:9–10). Throughout our exploration of God as spirit, we have faced the ambiguity of the word *ruach*. Once again, we ask: is *ruach* here wind, breath, or spirit? In this case, we find it is all three: it begins as the four winds, it is then breathed into the bones, and finally it possesses the power of spirit to bring bodies to life.

God then orders Ezekiel to prophesy to the people: "I will put My *ruach* into you and you shall live again, and I will set you upon your own soil. Then you shall know that I the Eternal have spoken and have acted" (37:14). Radak, Rabbi David Kimchi, writing in the twelfth century, wants to know, why would God promise to put God's *ruach* into the people after already reviving them with *ruach*? He concludes that this second reference must mean a different kind of *ruach*, just as it did for creation and revelation—the *ruach* that enables us to live and the *ruach* that enables us to understand. "This is the spirit of intelligence," Radak says, "which God will inject after raising up the dead from the grave. . . . God promises the people that He will instill in them knowledge, understanding, and wisdom."[57] For Rabbi David Altschuler, writing in the eighteenth century, the spirit that God promises is not merely the spirit of understanding, but God is saying, "I shall restore to you the spirit of prophecy."[58] The people will be able to hear God's voice, respond to God's will, and fulfill their partnership with the divine. According to Altschuler, this is a promise of Moses' wish back in the wilderness, "Would that all God's people were prophets!"

In Ezekiel's vision, it is God's spirit that will enable us to return from exile closer to God than ever before. Exile has been a central theme in Jewish history—from the Assyrian exile to the Babylonian exile to the Roman exile, which lasted for almost two thousand years until the founding of the modern state of Israel in 1948, the Jewish people have spent most of our existence away from home. The exile takes place on a number of levels: exile from land, exile from each other (as we were dispersed in the Diaspora across the world), and exile from God.

If Sinai was a great wedding, the exile felt like a divorce. We, the Jewish people, and God are separated from one another, and longing for return. The return of which the prophets speak is multilayered. It includes return to the land, the gathering of the people from the four corners of the earth, and the return to God, such that one day, all people will be prophets able to hear and understand what God wants of us.

According to the Kabbalists, the exile is not only between the Jewish people and God but also between God and God. God's masculine and feminine sides are in exile from one another, have turned their faces from one another. What it means to do *tikkun olam* ("repair of the world") is to do acts (*mitzvot*) that not only repair what is broken in the material world but also repair God, return God to Godself.

ZECHARIAH: BY SPIRIT ALONE

When Jews return from exile, how will we rebuild? If return from exile plays out on multiple levels—return to the land, return to each other, return to God, repair of God—what is the balance between physical effort and spiritual turning? What is the relationship between human strength and God's spirit? These are the questions raised by the prophet Zechariah.

On any given Shabbat morning, Jews all over the world read the same portion from the Torah. Each Shabbat we read the next weekly portion, or *parashah*, sequentially from the beginning of Genesis through to the end of Deuteronomy. In addition, each Shabbat we read the *haftarah*, or concluding reading, a portion from the Prophets that relates thematically to the Torah portion. On the first Shabbat of Chanukah, the eight-day festival of lights commemorating the rededication of the Temple after its destruction by the Syrian Greek emperor Antiochus, Jews read a *haftarah* selection from the prophet Zechariah. Zechariah lived in the sixth century BCE, in the time of the Persian Empire, and was part of the exile community that returned from Babylonia to Jerusalem to rebuild the Temple under the leadership of Zerubbabel.

As the people prepare to rebuild the Temple, Zechariah has a vision of the great *menorah*, a vision that links him to Chanukah. "I see a *menorah* of gold, with a bowl above it. The lamps on it are seven in number." As the Tabernacle, and the first Temple after it, had a menorah with seven lights, Zechariah's menorah represents the rekindling of the holy lights, signifying the rededication of the Temple.

Here's where God's spirit comes in. Zechariah is concerned that the people will renew the physical structure of the Temple and the sacrificial practices that take place within it but not realign their hearts or their actions. He is concerned that the people need not only a physical return but also a spiritual return from exile; not only a physical rebuilding of the Temple but also a spiritual turning to God. When Zechariah seeks the meaning of his vision of the menorah, the angel in the vision tells him: "Not by might, nor by power, but by My spirit—said Adonai of Hosts" (Zech. 4:6).

In Zechariah's vision, the rededication of the Temple would be accomplished not by human strength but by God's spirit. God's spirit, which gives us life through breath; God's spirit, which enables us to understand; God's spirit, which will redeem us from oppression and exile, will also enable us to rededicate our world to God's service and purpose.

Today, Zechariah's vision has been embraced by many Jews who see within it a message that the redemption of our world will not ultimately come through physical violence and force but through spiritual understanding and leadership. In this vision, God's spirit not only pushes us to change, not only gives us a vision of a world redeemed, but also provides an alternative to human might. In this contemporary reading of Zechariah, God's spirit is concerned not only with ends but also with means, not only with justice but also with peace.

MESSIAH AND THE MESSIANIC AGE

Throughout Israelite history, God's *ruach* rested on leaders who saved the people from defeat and despair. Beginning with the prophets, we see a claim that there will be an individual anointed by God who will bring redemption to Israel and the world. As we saw earlier, Isaiah proclaims that a future leader will be set apart by the *ruach* upon him: "The spirit of Adonai shall rest upon him: a spirit of wisdom and insight, a spirit of counsel and valor, a spirit of devotion and reverence for Adonai" (Isa. 11:2). "This is my servant, whom I uphold, My chosen one, in whom I delight. I have put My spirit upon him, he shall teach the true way to the nations" (Isa. 42:1). "The spirit of Adonai God is upon me, because Adonai has anointed me; he has sent me as a herald of joy to the humble, to bind up the wounded of heart, to proclaim release to the captives, liberation to the imprisoned" (Isa. 61:1).

Many interpreters understand these passages as references to the messiah. In Midrash Rabbah, the great collection of rabbinic midrash redacted in the sixth century, the rabbis go so far as to say that every reference to *ruach Elohim* in Torah is a reference to messiah—that the spirit of God is messiah: "From the time of creation constant reference is made in holy writ to messiah and the messianic hope of Israel. The spirit of God moved upon the face of the waters'; the spirit of God means messiah."[59] In the Jewish understanding, the messiah has not yet come, for redemption has not yet come to Israel and the world. However, even more than the prophets speak of a personal messiah, they speak of a messianic age, in which a universal spirit enters all people and returns us to God. On that day, all of humanity will feel God's spirit upon us. And every person, without distinction, will know God: "For all of them from the least of them to the greatest, shall know me, declares Adonai" (Jer. 31:34).

"Even as I pour water on thirsty soil, and rain upon dry ground, so will I pour My spirit on your offspring" (Isa. 44:3). "And this shall be my covenant with them, said Adonai: My spirit which is upon you, and the words which I have placed in your mouth, shall not be absent from your mouth, nor from the mouth of your children, nor from the mouth of your children's children—said Adonai—from now on, for all time" (Isa. 59:21). In this vision, all of our children's children will be prophets, their mouths full of God's words, their thirsty bodies full of God's spirit. As Hermann Cohen says it, "There may be an individual messiah, but he will be surrounded by a nation, and a world, that is immersed in God's spirit and ready to redeem the world with him."[60]

We will turn to the person with whom we think we have nothing in common, we will turn to our enemies, and we will see God's spirit within them, that they too are created in the image of God. We will see the person with the little cardboard sign on the side of the road and invite him into our house, and we will know that we are safe. No one will harm another, so that we will open the doors of our prisons and close our battered-women's shelters. No child will grow up to serve in an army, to kill or be killed. Expanding on Isaiah's vision that we will beat our swords into plowshares and our spears into pruning hooks, the poet Yehuda Amichai imagines that after our swords are plowshares and our spears are pruning hooks, we will keep beating so that anyone who wants to make swords or spears has to make plowshares or pruning hooks first.

In a midrash, Elijah, the herald of the messiah who had so much *ruach* that his disciple Elisha asked to receive a double portion of his master's spirit, says, "I call to witness heaven and earth: whether Israelite or Gentile, man or woman, manservant or maidservant: the holy spirit dwells in all, according to their deeds."[61] In other words, the holy spirit, rather than representing God or a singular messiah, is a gift that will be bestowed on all humanity, inspiring and enabling us to redeem the world. We saw that when the psalmist pleads that God not take the holy spirit away, he is yearning for the feeling of closeness to God's presence. We saw that when the midrash speaks of Saul and David receiving holy spirit, it is a conduit enabling them to discern how to live a good life. When Maimonides describes the holy spirit descending on a person, it is God's spirit that inspires eloquence. When Malbim speaks of the holy spirit resting on us in the messianic age, it gives us the power of prophecy. In each case, the holy spirit is synonymous with God's spirit, a gift from God that touches humanity, giving us a sense of connection to the divine and gifts of discernment, eloquence, and, in messianic times, the power of prophecy.

God's spirit is right at the center of Judaism's prophetic vision for redemption. God's spirit moves our prophets to speak and fills their mouths with prophecy. God's spirit is with us when we are in exile and with us when we return home. In the era when the world is redeemed, God's spirit will guide our messiah and, more important, open all of us to God.

10
Spirit in Action Today

E HAVE SEEN IN TANAKH THAT GOD'S spirit causes us to live and to understand why we are alive. God's spirit was there to free the Hebrews from Egypt, and God's spirit empowered the Hebrew prophets to speak and gave them visions. In their visions, the world will be redeemed through God's spirit. God's spirit will guide not only the messiah but will also pour out on all of us until we are filled with it.

We now look at how God's spirit helps us get from here to there. Standing in the broken world of today, holding out this vision of our world redeemed, we turn to God's spirit to help us move forward.

What is the force inside of us that motivates us to change the world? What is the impulse that pulls us to do something? If we are designed for survival, as evolutionary theory suggests, how does the expenditure of calories to assist someone on the side of the road or the other side of the world contribute to our survival? A hungry child in Haiti or sweatshop worker in Bangladesh has no bearing on my survival. In fact, any diversion of my resources—energy, time, money—to that child or worker weakens my comparative position and that of my children. What is it, then, that moves us to believe that the child's suffering is not inevitable, to believe that there is something that we can do about it, and to feel motivated to act to change the outcome?

In order to explain this phenomenon, we must admit to some ability within the human spirit to see from a perspective beyond the self. Remember when we learned about Balaam, the prophet who was assigned to curse the people Israel but instead suddenly saw them as deserving of blessing? Like Balaam, we all have the capacity to see from an elevated perspective, the perspective of universality, and to identify with it. Because God's spirit is in us, we are linked with transcendence, and this enables us to care.

However, this phenomenon requires not only elevated perspective, not only identification beyond the self, but also belief in change. Belief in change is even more challenging than identification with the suffering of others. We can see evidence of the suffering of others in real time—we don't have to imagine anything other than what our senses tell us. With digital photography, we can instantly capture an image of suffering human beings on the other side of the world. It is happening now, and we can see it.

Believing in change requires not only an elevated perspective, moving from "me" to "us," but also imagination across time. Change is always happening, though it is very difficult for us to perceive. Our children grow before our eyes, but rarely can we understand it. The seasons change; our cities and our societies change. Only when we can see from a perspective that transcends time can we know change is inevitable.

This is what spirit gives us: by linking us with the perspective of the Eternal, transcending both time and space, spirit has the potential to motivate us to act for change. This is what Ezekiel means by "a new heart and a new spirit" and what Joel and Isaiah mean when they speak of God's spirit pouring out on us—the ability to see beyond our own small lives, to rejoice in the triumphs of others, to hear and feel the suffering of others, to pine and to act for an end to that suffering.

FORCE OF CHANGE

This tug within us is the spirit of God, *yod-hey-vav-hey* (named in the Hebrew Bible with these four letters), "Being/Becoming," the force moving from what is to what can be. God's spirit is the force that gives us the taste of universality, the inkling that there is something beyond ourselves worth identifying with. As we learned, Jews are taught that our *neshamah* leaves us each night to rejoin God, to see the world from God's perspective. When it returns to us, we retain a whiff of eternality, a whiff of universality. This is the perspective of God—eternality and universality. It is our spirits that free us from the prisons of our selves—our tiny worlds of getting and doing—allowing us to see the wide open spaces and forever vistas of the Eternal Sovereign of All the Worlds.

Mordecai Kaplan, the founder of the Reconstructionist movement in contemporary Judaism, says it this way: "When we say that God is Process, we select, out of the infinite processes in the universe, that complex of forces and relationships which makes for the highest fulfillment of man as a human being and identify it by the term 'God.'"[62] Kaplan continues, "God is in the love which protects, creates, forgives. His is the spirit which broods upon the chaos men have wrought, disturbing its static wrongs, and stirring into life the formless beginnings of the new and better world."[63] In short, for Kaplan, God is "the power that makes for salvation."

WE MATTER

But even if we believe in change, there is another hurdle to leap in order to act. I need to believe that my actions matter, the effort of just one individual in 6.5 billion people on this planet. When we see with *ruach*, from the perspective of universality, our vision grows. The more our vision grows, the better we are able to grasp the magnitude of our world. The more accurately we see the magnitude of our world, the smaller our opinion of our own importance. This is a wisdom developed from *ruach*, from our ability to see from the perspective of universality, but it is only part of the story. As we learned from Jacob and his gifts, Jewish tradition also teaches that each of our lives is worth the whole world entire, that the world was created so that each of us might come into it. Therefore, the world needs us. God needs us. We would not be here if we were not needed.

And what are we needed to do? Actions that restore our relationship with God and each other. In the language of Judaism, these are *mitzvot*. The book of Leviticus is centered on the idea that the cosmos is in a delicate balance. Everything in the cosmos, down to the smallest detail, is in an interrelated and interdependent system. Through our actions every day—through error and willful transgression—human beings tip the system ever so slightly out of balance. In Leviticus, the Israelites bring sacrifices to restore balance. This teaches us that our actions matter—they heal and they harm. Though we are a tiny detail in the wondrous tapestry of creation, what we do counts.

After the destruction of the Temple, Jews could no longer bring animal sacrifices as a way to restore balance in the universe. The system was adapted for a dispersed, primarily urban population. What remained, though, was the conviction that every little move makes a difference—not only in the realms we can see and observe but also in realms beyond our powers of observation and understanding. The system is profoundly interconnected, and we are a part of it. Every little action we take, every word we speak, makes a difference. This is the system of *mitzvot*.

When simple logic seems to tell me that saying a blessing before and after I eat makes no difference at all, Judaism says it matters. When I ask myself, what difference will it make if I pay my gardener on the same day he works? Judaism insists that it matters. When I think, no one will know if I work on Shabbat, Judaism argues that these actions affect the world in ways we can and cannot see.

Today humanity is just beginning to understand that this is true in certain realms. We know now that we are profoundly interconnected with our ecosystem, and actions that seemed harmless before, because we could not observe their effect and because we could not conceive of their complex relation to the living systems around us, are in fact quite harmful. As chaos theory develops, we learn more and more about the complex interrelations among actions and reactions, causes and effects.

The prophets speak of the connection between our relationship with God and our relationship with human beings. No grand ritual can make up for fraud in the courts or deceptive weights and measures in the marketplace. Every detail of unethical action is heavy enough to destroy the world. The Kabbalists too taught that everything we do matters—every word we pray, every bit of our speech to one another, every action we take every day. They taught that every *mitzvah* we do is a *tikkun*, an act of repair on the broken world and an act of repair in the brokenness within God. Today many Jews speak of *tikkun olam* as a guiding principle for action—an abiding belief that it is incumbent upon us to repair the world with our own hands. The messiah will only come when we have done the work to bring about the messianic age.

ON THAT DAY YOUR NAME WILL BE ONE

The Jewish people proclaim our central statement of faith twice a day. *Shema Yisrael Adonai Eloheinu Adonai Echad.* "Hear O Israel, Adonai our God, Adonai is One." It is a statement of belief and a statement of aspiration. It is a belief that all we see, everything in creation, comes from a single source, that there is a fundamental unity in the universe called God. It is also an aspiration that one day all of the disparate, broken pieces will come together as one, all turning, each in our own ways, toward God.

In his prophecies, Zechariah envisioned the messianic age in the language of oneness, language that has found its way into every prayer service of the Jewish people, morning, noon, and night. At the end of the Aleinu prayer, we speak of a day when all of the nations will turn toward God. "On that day Adonai will be One, and his name will be One."

We wait, yearning and acting with all of our might to bring the time when God's unity and sovereignty will be visible to all people. As we grow in awareness of God's spirit within and around us, listening for our purpose and working for repair, this is what it means to aspire for wholeness. To see how broken the world is, and not to look away. To stand between the reality and the dream, unwilling to ignore the former or give up on the latter. God's spirit gives us the awareness of the reality and the vision of the world redeemed.

It is the spirit within us that waits for the day when *yod-hey-vav-hey*'s justice will come to reign on earth. It is the spirit within us that prompts us to act to bring that day about. It is our spirit that seeks to unite with the spirit of Adonai, the force of possibility, the eternal promise of becoming.

Each spring, during the holiday of Passover, when Jews from all walks of life gather around their seder tables, we leave a full cup of wine on the table for the prophet Elijah, the one who will herald the messianic age. At some point toward the end of the seder, a child will run to open the front door, that Elijah may enter, and a parent may drain the cup to convince the children that the hope of the messianic age is on its way. The very last words we say each year to close our seder speak of return. *L'shana haba'ah b'Yerushalayim* "Next year in Jerusalem!" Even those living in Jerusalem say these words, for they are speaking of a different Jerusalem, in which all are infused with God's spirit; a Jerusalem redeemed from warfare and struggle, one shining with God's spirit of justice and peace, a beacon to all nations, a hope for all peoples.

Postscript
Return

CREATION. REDEMPTION. REVELATION. JUDAISM IS A story, and we have journeyed from the beginning to the middle to the end: from the first words in the book of Genesis to commentaries of the modern day, from the birth of the cosmos to visions of the world to come. We have seen that God as spirit is everywhere in Judaism—at the first moments of creation, in the messianic age, and every day in between. We saw in the Hebrew Bible that we are born with God's spirit and wake into a world created through God's spirit. We saw that God's spirit gives us inspiration and understanding: awareness of the miracles that surround us and a sense of our purpose in the world. It is God's spirit that moves us toward a messianic future, a just and peaceful world brought nearer through our deeds. God's spirit rested on Hebrew kings and prophets, artisans and judges. We saw God's spirit in Egypt, the wilderness, and the Promised Land, in Psalms, Proverbs, Ecclesiastes, and Job. We saw God's spirit pull the Jewish exiles out of despair and return them to God. God's spirit is upon us, within us, and beyond us—as we live, learn, and strive to be who we are meant to be.

Just as Tanakh begins with God's spirit, Tanakh ends with God's spirit. Just as we find *ruach* in the second verse of the first chapter of Genesis, we find *ruach* in the second-to-last verse of the last chapter of 2 Chronicles. Ever since the tenth century, when it took on its present order, the Hebrew Bible concludes with God rousing the spirit of Cyrus, ruler of Persia, enabling the Israelites to rise up and return home (2 Chron. 36:22).

"I gather them back into their land and leave none of them behind. I will never again hide my face from them, for I will pour out My spirit upon the House of Israel, declares the Eternal God" (Ezek. 39:28–29). This is the conclusion of Israel's story; this is the promise that lies before us. No matter how profound our alienation, no matter how complete our exile, no matter how far we have turned away, no matter how far God may have turned away, we will turn back toward one another. We will return.

This is Judaism's promise for the world. This is how God as spirit—from a Jewish perspective—speaks to all people every-where. It is not you or I who return; it is a collective return. All of Israel, and the world collectively, will feel God's spirit upon us, will feel a new heart in our chests, will know ourselves to be awakened and sensitized and newly capable of return. And then, and then it will be God's spirit that enables us to serve God in the redemption of the whole world.

Every nation is chosen in its own way; every people hears its calling in a different voice. Every people is needed for the healing and redemption of our world. This is how Israel hears our mission: to turn toward God so that God can turn toward us.

On the High Holy Days in the fall, Jews all over the world focus on a process called *teshuvah*, meaning "return." We know that in small and large ways we have turned away. We have turned away from what we know to be right. We have turned away from God. We have spoken to others in ways that harmed them. We have acted, or failed to act, in ways that caused injury. We have participated in collective systems of economics and politics and international affairs that have cost lives and caused suffering. We have been silent witnesses and accomplices to hunger and homelessness, inequality and corruption.

On Rosh Hashanah and Yom Kippur we call ourselves to account for all that we have done and all that we have not done that fell short of the highest standards for how we know we should live. In directly repairing what we have done wrong, and then atoning for it, we return to God. Each year, we enact our personal and collective return from exile.

As we see from this review of Jewish text and tradition, it is God's spirit, poured on us, that enables us to see clearly how we ought to live and the ways in which we have fallen short. It is God's spirit that sparks our feelings of sorrow at the harm we have done, and the feeling of hope that we can do better. On Yom Kippur, as we collectively name our transgressions for which we atone, we beat our breasts as if to awaken and tap feeling into the heart of flesh that Ezekiel has promised us as a gift of God's spirit. We commit ourselves to the mission that Isaiah has set before us: to act as God's servants in the redemption of the world, with God's spirit strengthening us to fulfill our role. But on the High Holy Days, these aspirations do not concern a distant messianic age. These aspirations concern the here and now, starting with ourselves: our own speech, our own action, the pattern of our own lives. These aspirations are for today, that we, so small yet touched by spirit, might be worthy of the life breath breathed into us. With wisdom and understanding we aspire to live the highest call of Torah. With hope and faith we speak and act and live for the healing and redemption of our world.

Acknowledgments

J WANT TO THANK MY MANY TEACHERS FROM HEBREW Union College Los Angeles whose words and ideas have become a part of me. Dr Rachel Adler, who advised me at the inception of the book; Rabbi Dr. Dvora Weisberg, my friend and teacher; and Rabbi Dr. Josh Garroway and Dr. Leah Hochman, who gave of their time early on and helped me to structure the book. Rabbi Richard Levy spent many hours graciously and sensitively reading the manuscript, offering invaluable feedback and insights. He is the best mentor anyone could wish to have —as a rabbi and as a human being. Dr. Tamara Cohn Eskenazi generously spent hours guiding me from beginning to end with phone calls from Paris, e-mails from Rome, and face-to-face time in Los Angeles. The insights here about the *adam*, the Holiness Code, the worldview of Leviticus, and much more are hers. Her wisdom, understanding, and knowledge know no bounds.

Thank you to Rabbi Ken Chasen and to my congregants and partners at Leo Baeck Temple who are always trying to see with fresh eyes, feel with soft hearts, and strive for the world we need.

On the day after I first met Rabbi Larry Kushner, he looked into my eyes and forcefully insisted that I write a book. He then suggested me to Jon Sweeney at Paraclete for this book.

He believed in me with such intensity that he convinced me I had no choice but to write. I can only repay him by one day championing another as he has championed me.

Thank you to Jon Sweeney at Paraclete Press for believing that Judaism has something to say about God as spirit and that Christians would want to know what it is. It has been a curious delight to explore this topic. Thank you, too, to Pamela Jordan, Sister Mercy Minor, Jenny Lynch, and everyone at Paraclete for bringing the project to fruition.

There are very few friends like Joell Hallowell. This book would not be here if it were not for her.

And then there is my family, of origin and creation: Mom, Dad, Ondi, David, and most of all Felicia, Benjamin, and Eitan, thank you for your *ruach*.

Notes

INTRODUCTION

1 Moses Maimonides, *Mishneh Torah*, Book One, Chapter One, in Isadore Twersky, ed., *A Maimonides Reader*, (Springfield, NJ: Behrman House, 1972), 44.

2 Lawrence Hoffman, *The Journey Home: Discovering the Deep Spiritual Wisdom of the Jewish Tradition* (Boston: Beacon Press, 2002), 6–7.

3 In Rifat Sonsino, *Six Jewish Spiritual Paths: A Rationalist Looks at Spirituality* (Woodstock, VT: Jewish Lights, 2000).

CHAPTER 1: SPIRIT SHAPING COSMOS

4 Everett Fox, trans., *The Five Books of Moses* (New York: Schocken, 1997) 13.

5 Rashi on Genesis 1:1.

6 Bradley Shavit Artson, "Vibrating Over the Face of the Deep: God's Creating and Ours," *The Reform Jewish Quarterly*, Central Conference of American Rabbis, 57, no. 1 (Winter 2010): 40–47.

7 Ibid.

8 *MidrashTanchuma*, *Tazria* 3 in Artson, "Vibrating Over the Face of the Deep," 40–47.

9 Rashi on Genesis 1.

10 Daniel Matt, *God and the Big Bang: Discovering Harmony Between Science and Spirituality* (Woodstock, VT: Jewish Lights, 1996), 19-20.

11 Ibid. I am indebted to Matt's scientific understanding and descriptions for this entire paragraph.

12 Ibid.

13 Ibid. I highly recommend Matt's book for a Kabbalistic interpretation of this science.

14 Shabbetai Donnolo, Sefer Hkhmoni, on *Sefer Yetsirah* 1:10; paraphrased by Shim'on Lavi, Ketem Paz (Djerba, Tunisia: Jacob Haddad, 1940; repr., Jerusalem: Ahavat Shalom, 1981), 1:49d, quoted in Matt, *God and the Big Bang*, 43.

CHAPTER 2: SPIRIT IN US

15 Hermann Cohen, *Reason and Hope*, ed. and trans. Eva Jospe (New York: Norton, 1971), 136.

16 Abraham J. Heschel, *The Insecurity of Freedom: Essays on Human Existence* (New York: First Noonday Press, 1967), 158.

17 Ibid.

18 Cohen, *Reason and Hope*, 134.

19 Notice that "my spirit/breath" is the word *neshamah*, whereas God's breath/spirit is *ruach*. This is a common pattern in Job.

CHAPTER 3: SPIRIT AS A WAY TO GOD

20 Abraham J. Heschel, *Man's Quest for God: Studies in Prayer and Symbolism* (Santa Fe: Aurora Press, 1998).

21 Cohen, *Reason and Hope*, 135.

22 Ibid., 134.

23 Heinz-Josef Fabry, "*rûah,*" in *Theological Dictionary of the Old Testament*, ed. G. Johannes Botterweck, Helmer Ringgren,

and Heinz-Jossef Fabry, trans. David Green (Grand Rapids: Eerdmans, 2004), 13:365–402.

CHAPTER 5: EXTRAORDINARY SPIRIT

24 Elliot B. Gertel, "The Holy Spirit in the Zohar," *The Reform Jewish Quarterly* 56, no. 4 (Fall 2009): 80–102.

25 Louis Ginzberg, *The Legends of the Jews*, 1:329, in Gertel, "Holy Spirit in the Zohar."

26 See Gertel, "Holy Spirit in the Zohar," 82.

27 Ginzberg, *Legends of the Jews*, 6:262n81, in Gertel, "Holy Spirit in the Zohar," 82.

28 Gertel, "Holy Spirit in the Zohar," 90.

29 Moses Mendelssohn, *Biur* on Exodus, in Nehama Leibowitz, *New Studies in Shemot* (Israel: Maor Wallach Press),679.

30 Ibid.

31 Yitzchak Elhanan Spektor, *Be'er Yitzchak* (Konigsberg, 1858) in Nehama Leibowitz, *New Studies in Shemot* (Israel: Maor Wallach Press), 677.

32 Agnes de Mille, *Martha: The Life and Work of Martha Graham* (New York: Vintage Books, 1992), 264.

33 Mendelssohn, *Biur* on Exodus, in Leibowitz, *New Studies in Shemot*, 679.

34 "Man Lifts Car to Save Child's Life," *Wichita Eagle*, December 19, 2009.

35 Annual Report, Summit County Red Cross, 2009.

36 Moses Maimonides, *The Guide for the Perplexed*, trans. M. Friedlander (New York: Dover, 1956), 45.1.

37 Alvin J. Reines, *Maimonides and Abrabanel on Prophecy* (Cincinnati: Hebrew Union College, 1970), xviii.

CHAPTER 6: ORDINARY SPIRIT

38 Nehama Leibowitz, *Studies in Bamidbar* (Israel: Maor Wallach Press), 126.

39 Martin Buber, *Moses* (New York: Humanity Books, 1998), 150.

40 Leibowitz, *Studies in Bamidbar*, 128.

41 Abraham J. Heschel, *The Insecurity of Freedom: Essays on Human Existence* (New York: First Noonday Press, 1967), 159.

42 Lawrence Kushner, *Jewish Spirituality: A Brief Introduction for Christians* (Woodstock, VT: Jewish Lights, 2001), 20.

43 Lawrence Kushner, *Eyes Remade for Wonder* (Woodstock, VT: Jewish Lights, 1998).

44 Gertel, "Holy Spirit in the Zohar," 90.

45 Maimonides, *Guide for the Perplexed*, 3.18.

CHAPTER 7: FINDING PURPOSE THROUGH SPIRIT

46 Gerald Friedlander, transl. *Pirkei d'Rabbi Eliezer*, (New York: Jewish Publication Society, 2004), chap. 1.

47 Ibid., chap. 2.

48 Nehama Leibowitz, *New Studies in Bereshit* (Israel: Maor Wallach Press), 412.

49 Aryeh Kaplan, *Handbook of Jewish Thought* (New York: Moznaim Publishing, 1990), 86–87.

CHAPTER 8: DELIVERANCE AND DEMAND: GOD'S REDEMPTIVE SPIRIT

50 Joan Nathan, "Bread of Freedom in Times of Despair," *New York Times*, April 16, 2008.

51 Levi Yitzhak of Berdichev, *Kidushat Levi, Beshallach*, 151.

52 Nehama Leibowitz, New Studies in Bereishit (Israel: Maor Wallach Press), 113.

53 Gunther Plant, ed. *The Torah: A Modern Commentary* (New York: Union of Reform Judaism), 112.

CHAPTER 9: THE ROLE OF SPIRIT IN PROPHECY

54 Abraham J. Heschel, *The Prophets* (New York: HarperCollins, 1969), 5.

55 Solomon B. Freehof, ed. *Book of Ezekiel*, (New York: Union of American Hebrew Congregations, 1978).

56 Ibid.

57 Moshe Eisemann, transl. *The Book of Ezekiel: A New Translation with a Commentary Anthologized from Talmudic, Midrashic, and Rabbinic Sources*, (New York: Mesorah Publications, 1977).

58 Ibid.

59 *Genesis Rabbah* 2; *Leviticus Rabbah* 14. H. Freedman, transl. (New York: Soncino Press, 1983).

60 Hermann Cohen, *Reason and Hope*, ed. and trans. Eva Jospe (New York: Norton, 1971), 122.

61 *Tanna de-vei Eliyahu*, quoted by Hermann Cohen, *Reason and Hope*, ed. and trans. Eva Jospe (New York: Norton, 1971), 153n12.

CHAPTER 10: SPIRIT IN ACTION TODAY

62 Mordecai M. Kaplan, *Questions Jews Ask: Reconstructionist Answers* (New York: Reconstructionist Press, 1966), 102–3, quoted in *Dynamic Judaism, the Essential Writings of Mordecai Kaplan*, Emanuel Goldsmith and Mel Scult, eds. (Fordham University Press, 1991), 74.

63 Kaplan, *Questions Jews Ask*, 101.

Glossary of Terms

adam: earth creature, the first human being.

Adonai: a placeholder for God's name said by Jews instead of the unpronounceable tetragrammaton.

chochmah: wisdom, the ability to learn from every person and apply that learning to how to live a good life.

covenant: collective partnership between God and a people, in this case the Jewish people.

da'at: knowledge, intimacy; can mean intimacy with God.

Elohim: God.

Hasidic: referring to a joyous, mystical movement in Judaism founded in the eighteenth century in Eastern Europe.

holiness: commitment to the stranger and the powerless.

Kabbalists: a school of Jewish mysticism centering in Safed, in northern Israel, in the sixteenth century.

lashon hara: literally, "the evil tongue." Speech that harms, and the name for the Jewish ethics of speech.

menorah: candelabra. The menorah in the Temple had seven lights.

Midrash: the entire body of Jewish texts that uses gaps, repetitions, and inconsistencies in Torah to expand upon the Biblical narrative and seek out deeper meaning within it.

mitzvot: commandments from God. There are 613 in Torah.

neshamah: soul, life breath.

nefesh: being, life, creature.

nishmat chayim: breath of life.

rabbi: literally, teacher. The leaders of the Jewish people from the destruction of the second Temple in 70 CE until modernity.

ruach: spirit, breath, wind.

ruach hakodesh: holy spirit, synonymous with God's spirit, a conduit between humanity and God.

Tanakh: the Hebrew Bible, including Torah, the Prophets, and the Writings, from Genesis to 2 Chronicles. Redacted in the second century CE.

Torah: the Five Books of Moses—Genesis, Exodus, Leviticus, Numbers, and Deuteronomy.

teshuvah: turning, returning, repentance. The goal of the High Holy Days, based in deep self-reflection, direct repair of harm done, and a commitment to change.

tetragrammaton: *yod-hey-vav-hey*, the Jewish people's intimate, unpronounceable four-letter name for God.

tevunah: understanding, the ability to internalize wisdom in one's heart, and to apply it to making connections and distinctions.

tikkun olam: repair of the world.

ABOUT PARACLETE PRESS

WHO WE ARE

Paraclete Press is a publisher of books, recordings, and DVDs on Christian spirituality. Our publishing represents a full expression of Christian belief and practice—from Catholic to Evangelical, from Protestant to Orthodox.

We are the publishing arm of the Community of Jesus, an ecumenical monastic community in the Benedictine tradition. As such, we are uniquely positioned in the marketplace without connection to a large corporation and with informal relationships to many branches and denominations of faith.

WHAT WE ARE DOING

BOOKS

Paraclete publishes books that show the richness and depth of what it means to be Christian. Although Benedictine spirituality is at the heart of all that we do, we publish books that reflect the Christian experience across many cultures, time periods, and houses of worship. We publish books that nourish the vibrant life of the church and its people—books about spiritual practice, formation, history, ideas, and customs.

We have several different series, including the best-selling Living Library, Paraclete Essentials, and Paraclete Giants series of classic texts in contemporary English; A Voice from the Monastery—men and women monastics writing about living a spiritual life today; award-winning literary faith fiction and poetry; and the Active Prayer Series that brings creativity and liveliness to any life of prayer.

RECORDINGS

From Gregorian chant to contemporary American choral works, our music recordings celebrate sacred choral music through the centuries. Paraclete distributes the recordings of the internationally acclaimed choir Gloriæ Dei Cantores, praised for their "rapt and fathomless spiritual intensity" by *American Record Guide*, and the Gloriæ Dei Cantores Schola, which specializes in the study and performance of Gregorian chant. Paraclete is also the exclusive North American distributor of the recordings of the Monastic Choir of St. Peter's Abbey in Solesmes, France, long considered to be a leading authority on Gregorian chant.

DVDS

Our DVDs offer spiritual help, healing, and biblical guidance for life issues: grief and loss, marriage, forgiveness, anger management, facing death, and spiritual formation.

Learn more about us at our Web site:
www.paracletepress.com,
or call us toll-free at 1-800-451-5006.

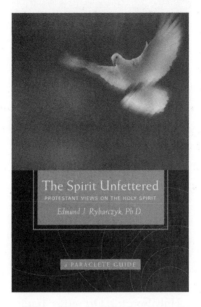

The Spirit Unfettered
Protestant Views on the Holy Spirit

by Edmund J. Rybarczyk

$15.99 Trade paperback ISBN: 978-1-55725-654-6

THIS CLEAR GUIDE WILL HELP YOU UNDERSTAND WHAT IS DISTINCTIVE about Protestant perspectives on who the Holy Spirit is and what the Holy Spirit does in our lives. The understandings of important historical theologians in the Protestant tradition such as Luther, The Anabaptists, Wesley and Barth as well as living theologians such as Jurgen, Moltmann, Wolfhart, Pannenberg, Clark, Pinnock, and Michael Welker are explored.

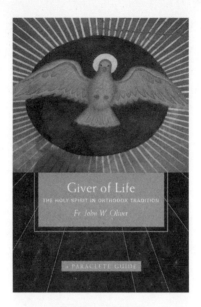

Giver of Life
The Holy Spirit in Orthodox Tradition

by Fr. John W. Oliver

$15.99 Trade paperback ISBN: 978-1-55725-675-1

GIVER OF LIFE LOOKS TO THE IMPRESSIVE BIBLICAL AND LITURGICAL
tradition of Orthodox Christianity, reflecting on the relationship
of the Holy Spirit to the Church, to the world, and to the human
person, Written with a poetic sensibility, this is a book weighty
in content but accessible in tone, not an academic study of the
mind, but a lived experience of the heart.

Available from most booksellers or through Paraclete Press:
www.paracletepress.com; 1-800 451-5006.
Try your local bookstore first.